Basic Bible Sermons on John

BASIC BIBLE SERMONS

ON

JOHN

Herschel H. Hobbs

BROADMAN PRESS
NASHVILLE, TENNESSEE

ISBN: 0-8054-2272-2
Dewey Decimal Classification: 226.5
Subject Heading: BIBLE. N.T. JOHN—SERMONS
Library of Congress Catalog Card Number: 89-48574

Printed in the United States of America

Unless otherwise indicated, Scripture is from the *King James Version*. Scripture quotations marked (NASB) are from the *New American Standard Bible.* © The Lockman Foundation, 1960, 1962, 1963, 1968, 1971, 1972, 1973, 1975, 1977. Used by permission. Scripture marked (NEB) is from *The New English Bible.* Copyright © The Delegates of the Oxford University Press and the Syndics of the Cambridge University Press, 1961, 1970. Reprinted by permission. Scripture marked (New Berkeley) is from *The Modern Language Bible, The New Berkeley Version.* Copyright 1945, 1959 © 1969 by Zondervan Publishing House. Used by permission.

Library of Congress Cataloging-in-Publication Data

Hobbs, Herschel H.
    Basic Bible sermons on John / Herschel H. Hobbs
      p. cm.
    ISBN 0-8054-2272-2
    1. Bible. N.T. John—Sermons. 2. Baptists—Sermons.
    3. Sermons, American. I. Title.
    BS2615.4.H63   1990
    252'.061—dc20 —dc20   89-48574
                                     CIP

To
FRANCES
who is now with the Lord—but who makes my lonely path brighter through the happy memories she left with me.

Contents

Other Books in the Basic Bible Sermons Series:

1
The Cosmic Christ

(John 1:1-18; Col. 1:15,17)

"In the beginning was the Word, and the Word was with God, and the Word was God. . . . All things were made by him; and without him was not any thing made that was made. . . . And the Word was made flesh, and dwelt among us, . . . full of grace and truth" (John 1:1,3,14).

Never were more majestic words penned. Never was so much grand truth stated in so few words. They introduce the simplest and profoundest of the Gospels. The purpose of this Gospel is "that ye might believe that Jesus is the Christ, the Son of God; and that believing ye might have life through his name" (20:31)

Jesus had a message for His contemporaries. But does He have a message for this space age? The purpose of this message is to show that He does.

The Background of John's Gospel

In order to understand any book one must know something of its background. John wrote this Gospel while in Ephesus. Primarily, its message was directed toward the Greeks.

In the first century A.D., there appeared a philosophy known as Gnosticism. Its name comes from the Greek word *gnōsis*, meaning "knowledge." Gnostics held that people were saved by advancing in knowledge.

Gnostics faced a problem in explaining the origin of the universe. They said God is absolutely good, and matter is absolutely evil. How, then, could such a God create such a universe? To their own satisfaction, at least, they imagined a series of beings coming out of God in descending order, each having less deity than the one above it. The lowest one had enough deity to create, but so little as to be able to create evil matter.

Coming in to contact with Christianity, Gnostics identified Christ as that lowest being. Thus they saw Him as a created being, a demigod, almost a demon since He created evil matter.

Furthermore, the Gnostics divided into two groups concerning Jesus Christ. The Docetic Gnostics (from *dokeō*, "I seem") said that Christ did not have a real flesh-and-blood body. He only *seemed* to have one. They denied the humanity of Christ. The Cerinthian Gnostics (from their leader Cerinthus) held that Christ neither was born, nor did He die. Deity came upon Jesus at His baptism and left Him on the cross. So they denied the deity of Jesus. These views cut through Christology. It is as great a heresy to deny Christ's humanity as to deny Jesus' deity. So both Paul, in Colossians, and John, in his Gospel and 1 John, wrote to refute this heresy.

Gnostics are still with us, for anyone who denies either Jesus' deity or Christ's humanity is a neo-Gnostic. It is our purpose, therefore, to look at Jesus Christ in three relationships: to God, to the natural order, and to us.

Christ's Relation to God

"In the beginning was the Word, and the Word was with God, and the Word was God" (John 1:1).

"In the beginning"—whenever that was. These three words throw us back to Genesis 1:1. As the Bible opens its account of God's creative work, so John begins his account of the beginning of God's redemptive work in Christ. Revelation 13:8 speaks of Christ as slain before the foundation of the world. So, in effect, the redemptive work fixed in eternity was wrought out in time that we might believe in Him who was slain for our sins.

John personified "Word" *(logos)*. This means the open, spoken manifestation of the speaker. And "in the beginning" gives us a clue as to John's selection of "Word." In Genesis 1, each new phase of God's creative work is introduced with "and God said." There is His open, spoken manifestation. So, as in the beginning God spoke the universe into being, in Christ He spoke His final word of revelation—redemption—in the person of His Son, Jesus Christ.

"Was" is the verb "to be" expressing essential, and in this case, eternal being. It may read "always was." There had never been a time when Christ did not exist. Like God the Father, He is eternal in nature and being.

Furthermore, Christ always was "with God." Literally, He was "face-to-face with God." In ancient times, let us say, a person entertained two rulers. One was tall, the other was short. The host had to seat the shorter one on pillows so that when they looked at one another, it was on an even line. Neither looked up or down at the other. We would say that they saw *eye to eye*. This expressed equality. To express it, the same phrase was used as here. So "the Word [always] was [equal] with God." There is no gradation in the Godhead.

Likewise, literally translated, the final phrase should read, "and the Word [Christ] always was God Himself." For "God was in Christ, reconciling the world unto himself" (2 Cor. 5:19).

Thus in one terse sentence, John answered the Gnostics, then and now, by declaring the coeternity, coequality, and coexistence of Christ with God the Father.

Now let us turn to Colossians 1:15 where Paul said that Christ "is the image of the invisible God." "Image" means "exact manifestation." This does not mean that God is visible but has not been seen. It means that He cannot be seen with the natural eye. "God is a Spirit," said Jesus (John 4:24). And a spiritual being cannot be seen by the natural eye. This is the reason for the incarnation: So that Jesus could say, "He that hath seen me hath seen the Father" (John 14:9).

When my wife was living, I bore three relationships to her. I was her husband, the father of her child, and her pastor. I was not three distinct people. I was one person, but I bore three relationships to her. While no human example adequately illustrates the Godhead, this shows how it is possible to be one, yet bear three relationships to another. In Jesus Christ, God revealed Himself as our Redeemer.

Christ's Relationship to the Natural Order

Literally, John 1:3 reads, "Every single thing in the universe through him became [came into being], and apart from him became not even one thing which became."

Christ is the intermediate agent in the creative work. He created the universe from atoms to solar systems!

Note the change from the verb "to be" to the verb "to become." Christ is eternal. But through Him something that did not exist came into being. Thus, John denied the eternity of matter.

Turning again to Colossians, Paul said that Christ is "the firstborn of every creature" (Col. 1:15). Of course, the New Testament was written in Greek. Long before I could read the Greek New Testament, I said that that is not what Paul meant, for it makes Christ a created being, the very idea that the apostle was refuting. "Firstborn" means just that in Luke 2:7 where Mary "brought forth her firstborn son." Later, she had other children by Joseph. But here—no!

In my library I have the nine-volume set of Gerhard Kittel's *Theological Dictionary of the New Testament*. It is perhaps the most exhaustive work in its field. My only objection to it is that it tells me more than I want to know. But one day I decided to read what it says about the word translated "firstborn." I read page after page, much of it in fine print. Several times I was tempted to stop. But I am glad that I did not. Because the very last line said that the word was sometimes used in the sense of *prior being* with the meaning of "lordship." Kittel cited Colossians 1:15 as an example. And there it was! Paul said that Christ is "the Lord of all creation" (my translation).

But Paul was not through. In Colossians 1:17 he said, literally, "And He alone is before every single thing in the universe, and the universe as a whole in Him holds together." We speak of the law of gravity when we should speak of the law of Christ.

From earliest time, people spoke of a geocentric of earth-centered universe. The ancients thought that the sun moved about the earth. But Galileo proved that the earth moves about the sun. So we called it a heliocentric or sun-centered universe. However, we can no longer say that. Astronomers now tell us that what we once thought was the universe is only our solar system. We are told that there are innumerable solar systems, each with its own sun and billions of stars. One astronomer estimates that there are fourteen quadrillion such solar systems. That is fourteen followed by fifteen zeros. It stretches our minds even to think about it!

So, no longer can we say that we live in a heliocentric universe. If the sun is not the center of the universe, then who or what is? Writing under the inspiration of the Holy Spirit, Paul told us almost two thousand years ago. For, "the universe as a whole in Him holds together."

Thus we live in a Christocentric universe—not a *sun*-centered but a *Son*-centered universe!

In 1962 Frances and I were on a mission tour of Latin America. Landing in Porto Alegre, Brazil, I was interviewed by a newsman. Our nation was well into the space program. President Kennedy had predicted that we would land men on the moon by the end of that decade. The newsman noted that some people thought space exploration was a sin and wanted my opinion. I replied, "Exploring space is no more a sin than boring a hole in the ground to get water or oil. The possibility of sin lies in what we do with what we learn. The same oil well will produce gasoline for a car driven by a drunken driver who injures people. It also will produce gasoline for an ambulance to take the injured to a hospital."

Also, in 1973 I taught a term at Golden Gate Theological Seminary. One day the *San Francisco Chronicle* carried an article about two astronomers working in the large observatory there. They had picked up radio signals from an object in space. Their measuring instruments showed that it was fifty million light years from the earth, with light traveling at a speed of over 186,000 miles per second. Someone said that object may have burned up billions of years ago, but its radio waves were still coming through. The human mind can scarcely grasp it!

I do not understand this. But it does not frighten me. Regardless of how large science may calculate that the universe is, I know that my Lord made it all! *The more we learn about the universe, the greater do we understand the glory of Christ.*

And He keeps this vast universe running in exact precision. In our own solar system, we determine earth time by the movement of the heavenly bodies.

Many years ago we broke ground for the building of the Southern Baptist Radio and Television Commission in Fort Worth, Texas. Since I was "The Baptist Hour" preacher at the time, Paul Stevens, president of the Commission, asked me to be the speaker. I always told Paul that if they boiled him down to a pint, it would be a pint of imagination. In that business one needs such.

Well, Paul would not think of breaking ground with a shovel, not even a gold one. He said, "We are in the space business, and we must somehow use space in breaking ground." So he went to a firm in Fort Worth that was a part of the NASA program. After telling the man what he wanted to do, Paul was told to bury some dynamite at a safe distance from those attending the ground breaking. Then they would attach a telephone wire to the dynamite. The other end of the wire would be attached to a machine. The machine would be aimed at a place in the sky where a certain star would be at the moment the dynamite was to be detonated. At that moment light from that star would shine directly into the machine, creating a spark of electricity. The electricity would pass through the wire and detonate the dynamite. Through a telephone, officials would alert Paul as to the time.

On the specified day, the program was ahead of schedule. Paul told me that when he pulled my sleeve I was to stop talking for a couple of seconds. I did. And then—*boom!* The star was not a second early or late. It was right on time.

In this is a lesson for each of us. If the Lord can make this vast universe a cosmos instead of a chaos, surely He can take our shattered lives, put the pieces together, and give us orderly lives.

Christ's Relationship to Us

"The Word was made flesh, and dwelt among us, . . . full of grace and truth."

"Was made" translates the verb "to become" or come into being. "Dwelt" renders the verb meaning to live in a tent, a temporary dwelling. For thirty-three years, Christ became something He had never been before—a flesh-and-blood man. He identified Himself completely with us, apart from sin. He did so that He might reveal God's grace and truth in terms of our understanding.

We say that Jesus of Nazareth was God. And so He was. But to me a far more thrilling truth is that God became Jesus of Nazareth—for me!

Just think of it! He who always was, who always was equal with God, yes, who always was God Himself—who created the universe from atoms to multiplied solar systems, who is the Lord of creation, the center of the universe, and who keeps it running in exact precision—became a flesh-and-blood man for you and me!

Furthermore, He became obedient unto death, even the death of the cross, and He is alive forevermore that He might provide redemption to all who receive Him as Savior. And He would have done so, even if you were the only lost person in His universe.

The planets move at His word. Only you and I, made in God's image with the right of choice, can say yes or no to Him. But upon your choice hangs your eternal destiny.

John 1:11-12 says of Christ, "He came unto his own, and his own received him not. But as many as received him, to them gave he power to become the sons of God, even to them that believe on his name." Will you reject Him or receive Him? Only you can answer that question.

2
Up and Out

(John 3:1-21)

"Jesus answered and said unto him, Verily, verily, I say unto thee, Except a man be born again, he cannot see the kingdom of God. . . . Ye must be born again" (John 3:3,7).

A man living in a penthouse on Fifth Avenue can be as lost from God as can a man in the Bowery. Yet you will find no rescue missions on Fifth Avenue. We are so wedded to material things we sometimes forget that a person's economic or social status does not count with God. In Nicodemus we have a case of one who is *up and out*. He was up in the world, but he was out of the kingdom of God.

The Man, Nicodemus (John 3:1-2)

"Nicodemus" means "a conqueror of the people." Whether he conquered anyone else, Nicodemus won a victory within himself, but only after a struggle.

Nicodemus was a Pharisee, which means that he was a conservative in his theology. He accepted the Old Testament as the Word of God. He believed in angels, miracles, and the resurrection from the dead. He was the opposite of the Sadducees who accepted only the five books of Moses as Scripture and denied all the rest of the things mentioned above. We assume that as a good Pharisee, Nicodemus also lived by the meticulous and multitudinous rules devised by the rabbis for governing the conduct of one's life. Someone has called Nicodemus "the fairest flower of Judaism."

Also, Nicodemus was a man of prominence. He was "a ruler of the Jews." He was a member of the Sanhedrin, the supreme court of the Jews. Among all the Jews in Palestine, he was one of seventy men, plus the high priest, who comprised this august body. Under the Romans, this body had the final say in civic and religious matters. The Romans reserved to themselves the right of capital punishment. Jesus also called him a "teacher." To the Jews this was the supreme title (3:10). Nicodemus is the only member of the Sanhedrin who dared speak a word of defense for Jesus during His public ministry, an act which required great courage (7:50-52). And judging by the amount of myrrh and aloes he supplied for Jesus' burial, he must have been a man of wealth (19:39).

Yet, in spite of all these things, Nicodemus was outside the kingdom of God. He was a lost man. He was *up* in this life. But he was *out* insofar as eternal life was concerned.

Nicodemus "came to Jesus by night" (v. 2). Why "by night"? Was it because he did not want it known that he visited Jesus? Or that he knew where to find Him at that time? More likely, he came at night in order to have an uninterrupted visit with Jesus. At the Passover season, Jerusalem and its vicinity was crowded with pilgrims. Such a visit would be impossible during the day.

The Dialogue (John 3:2-15)

Note that Nicodemus opened the dialogue with a compliment for Jesus. "Rabbi, we know that thou art a teacher come from God" (v. 2). Otherwise, no man could do the signs that He did (2:23). "Know" means to have perceptive knowledge. Nicodemus had thought the matter through and had concluded that Jesus was from God.

For Nicodemus to call Jesus a rabbi was the supreme compliment among the Jews. Especially, since Jesus was not an accredited teacher among them. Is "we" editorial? Or did Nicodemus come as a representative of other members of the Sanhedrin? Either is possible. It is possible that John did not record the entire conversation, but, at least, he gave the heart of it.

In any case, Jesus took no note of Nicodemus's compliment. Instead, He used shock treatment on him. "Verily, verily, I say unto thee, Except a man be born again, he cannot see the kingdom of

God" (v. 3). In John's Gospel, "verily, verily" always introduces a solemn statement by Jesus. Had Jesus said that Gentiles must be born again, Nicodemus would have said, "Amen." Jews regarded Gentiles as being outside the mercy of God. One rabbi said they were but fuel for the fires of hell.

But as a Jew, Nicodemus thought that he was already in the kingdom of God. Imagine, therefore, his shock to hear that he must be born again even to see—let alone be in—the kingdom of God. To see means to see with perception. We would use *perceive:* to see through, to understand the kingdom of God.

Even today some people have strange ideas about what it means to be a Christian. Many years ago the Southern Baptist Radio and Television Commission made a series of television programs called "Christ Is the Answer." Paul Stevens insisted that in every film the characters having part in the message were to be Christians.

One day he and the director were selecting people to play these roles. When they had finished, Paul asked, "Are all these people Christians?" The director replied, "Certainly! Every one of them is an American citizen!"

He held the same mistaken notion as Nicodemus. Being an American citizen no more makes a person a Christian than being a Jew makes one a part of God's kingdom.

In light of Jesus' words, Nicodemus expressed his surprise. "How can a man be born when he is old? can he enter the second time into his mother's womb, and be born?" (v. 4).

Obviously, Jesus was thinking of a spiritual birth, while Nicodemus thought of a second physical birth. In fact, the Greek word for "again" (*anōthen*) may mean that, or it can mean "from above." Apparently, Jesus chose this word for that very reason. He had to lead Nicodemus away from the idea that his natural birth meant he was already in the kingdom. He wanted him to understand that a spiritual birth from above was necessary. Being born to Christian parents does not make a child a Christian.

Jesus introduced His answer with the words "verily, verily" (vv. 3,5,11). "Except a man be born of water and of the Spirit, he cannot enter into the kingdom of God. That which is born of the flesh is flesh; and that which is born of the Spirit is spirit. Marvel not that I say unto you, Ye must be born again" (vv. 5-7).

What did Jesus mean by "born of water"? Some see it as baptismal regeneration. Others see it, along with "Spirit," as spiritual cleansing. But we must interpret it in context. The problem here is the difference between natural and spiritual births.

Everyone familiar with the natural birth knows that it is accompanied by water. Obviously, the spiritual birth is accompanied by the Holy Spirit. Thus Jesus reminded Nicodemus of the difference between the two: "born of the flesh is flesh," and "born of the Spirit is spirit." So, actually verse 5 is like a piece of meat between two slices of bread (vv. 4,6).

By the fleshly birth, a person is born into a natural family with natural relationships and responsibilities. One born of the Spirit is born into a spiritual family with spiritual relationships and responsibilities. In verse 7, "marvel" renders a verb meaning "to wonder without understanding." So, literally, Jesus said, "Stop wondering without understanding that I said, It is morally and spiritually necessary [dei] you to be born again [from above]."

Nicodemus's problem was that he was reaching out for *understanding* rather than *faith*. If we understand something, it is not through faith.

Jesus often taught from spur-of-the-moment events. It is possible that at that very moment a breeze began to rustle the leaves of a nearby olive tree. In effect, Jesus said, "Do you hear that, Nicodemus? That movement of the leaves is caused by a breeze. Do you see the breeze? Or do you understand it?" Of course, neither was true. Nicodemus knew the breeze was there only by the effect of its power and presence.

The ancients formed their language out of experience. They experienced an invisible force in nature, either a gentle breeze or a tornado. They called it *pneuma*. They recognized an invisible force (breath) in humans and animals. They also called it *pneuma*. Likewise, they saw a power in human religious experience, and they called it *pneuma*. Thus, depending upon the context, *pneuma* may mean any of these: wind, breath, or spirit.

So Jesus chose this figure to try leading Nicodemus to comprehend the spiritual birth, the birth from above. "The wind [*pneuma*] bloweth where it listeth [wishes], and thou hearest the sound thereof, but canst not tell whence it cometh, and whither it goeth; so is every one that is born of the Spirit [*pneuma*]" (v. 8). G. Campbell Morgan suggested that this may well read, "The Spirit works as He wills." We do not see the wind. But we accept it because we see its results. In like manner, we do not see the Holy Spirit. But we see the results of His work. We may well think of the Holy Spirit as the attending physician as each soul is born into the kingdom of God.

However, Nicodemus was so wedded to the natural that still he did not comprehend the spiritual. So he said, "How can these things be?" (v. 9). He did not understand the figure of the wind, so how could he grasp the deeper things of the Spirit?

But Nicodemus was an expert in the Jewish Scriptures. So Jesus resorted to them (vv. 14-15). He cited the episode of the fiery serpents (Num. 21:6-9). When the people cried out to Moses for help, Jehovah told him to make a serpent of brass, hold it up, and everyone who looked upon it lived. Apparently for the first time, a small light of understanding appeared upon Nicodemus's face. He recognized the passage to which Jesus referred.

Then Jesus related it to Himself. "Even so must the Son of man be lifted up: That whosoever believeth in him should not perish, but have eternal life."

In John "lifted up" refers to Jesus' crucifixion, something of which Nicodemus knew nothing at this point. At the same time Jesus introduced the element of faith. Why were the Israelites saved from the serpent bites? Because of the element of which the brass serpent was made? Or because of the excellence of the workmanship in making the serpent? Or because of the graceful way in which Moses held the serpent? All these questions call for a negative answer. They were saved simply because the people had faith in God's promise.

Likewise you will be saved from sin only through faith in God's promise to save all who believe in His crucified and risen Son. Moses' act of lifting up the serpent did not heal all the Israelites. Only those were healed who responded to God's promise in faith. Neither are all people saved from the penalty of sin because Jesus was crucified. Only those are saved who exercise faith in the crucified One.

"Whosoever" includes you, me, and all others who respond through faith in the Savior. "Perish" renders the word akin to Apollyon, the destroyer, one name of the devil. It might well read "cast into hell." And "eternal life" or "age-abiding life" is not quantitative, a life received at physical death. It is qualitative, a quality of life received the moment we believe in Jesus and that abides in eternity.

Some preach a message that says you will not know that you are saved until the final judgment. The gospel is that you can be saved here and now and know it. Many times prayers are closed with the plea, "And save us in heaven at last." Well, my friend, unless you are saved now by grace through faith in Jesus, you will not be saved "in heaven at last."

The Purpose of the Incarnation (John 3:16-18)

Some interpreters feel Jesus' conversation with Nicodemus ended with John 3:15. They hold that John 3:16-21 is the apostle's commentary. I see the whole as Jesus' words. It is because of people's lost condition that God became Jesus of Nazareth.

"For God so loved the world, that he gave his only begotten Son, that whosoever believeth in him should not perish, but have everlasting life" (3:16).

This is the best known and most often quoted verse in the Bible. Yet seldom is John 3:16 used as a sermon text, because when we quote it, we have said it all. It is the "little Gospel" or the gospel in superlatives. The best commentary on it is found in Philippians 2:6-11.

John 3:16 presents the greatest Lover: "God." It expresses the greatest degree of love: "so loved." It includes the greatest object of love: "the world." It shows the greatest expression of love: "he gave." And the greatest gift of love: "his only begotten Son." It depicts the greatest response to love: "whosoever believeth in him." It declares the greatest deliverance of love: "should not perish." And it presents the greatest result of love: "but have everlasting life."

In the Greek text, this verse opens with the word for "so." It shows the kind of love God has for a lost world. First Peter 1:18-19 says, "Forasmuch as ye know that ye were not redeemed with corruptible things, as silver and gold, . . . But with the precious blood of Christ, as of a lamb without blemish and without spot." If you could have been redeemed by silver and gold, God could have given mountains of such and have had mountains of it left over. But He had to give all of something that He had. He has only one Son. So He gave Him to provide redemption from your sins.

But to me the principal word in this verse is "whosoever." Literally it means, "every single one of the whole, the ones believing in him." I am so thankful for "whosoever." For "whosoever meaneth me!"

"Have," literally, reads "may have." This suggests the possibility that one may not come to have age-abiding life. The fact that Jesus provided this life does not mean that everyone automatically has it. It is available, but only to the ones who believe in Jesus. But "every single one of the whole" means that Christ would have paid the price of redemption—even if you or I had been the only lost sinners in the world.

Verses 17-18 stress the individual nature of salvation. "Condemn" should read "judge." The purpose of the incarnation was not that the Son should judge the world. It was that through Him the world might be saved. (At His second coming He will judge the world.) Those believing in Him are not judged. They have already been judged in Christ who died for their sins. But the ones not believing in Him already are judged (perfect tense, a fixed, completed state). Why? Not because they are such terrible sinners. Rather, they are judged because they have not believed (perfect tense again, has not and does not believe, a fixed state) in the only begotten Son of God.

So, the one sin that will send your soul to hell is a fixed refusal to believe in Jesus as your Savior. You can believe in Him, if you will to do so. Ralph Waldo Emerson said that we bear faith as an apple tree bears apples. It is our very nature to believe. But in what or in whom do we believe? The only way to be saved is through our personal faith in Jesus Christ (Acts 4:12).

Many years ago I preached a sermon on "What Must You Do to Be

Lost?" My text was John 3:18. We hear many sermons on what we must do to be saved. But what about to be lost?

My conclusion is that you need not do anything to be lost. Because of your sins you are lost already.

So your problem is not how to be lost but how to be saved. I was saved at eleven years of age. The preacher's text was Pilate's question, "What shall I do then with Jesus which is called Christ?" (Matt. 27:22). That is your all-important question. How will you answer? Upon your answer hangs your eternal destiny.

3
Down and Out

(John 4:1-42)

"There cometh a woman of Samaria to draw water" (John 4:7).

Can you think of a less-inspiring text for a sermon? In Palestine, carrying water was/is a woman's work. In late afternoon as you drive along the roads of Palestine, you can still see women with their water pots on their shoulders. A woman to draw water! So commonplace! Such drudgery!

Yet this simple statement introduces us to one of the most dramatic episodes in the life of Jesus. In it we see the master soul-winner at work.

In John 3, we see Jesus dealing with a man who was *up and out*. In John 4, we see Him dealing with a woman who was *down and out*. As Nicodemus represents one in the highest level of society, in this woman we see one at its lowest level. Yet Jesus' heart went out to both of them. Both of these instances provide us case studies in the art of soul-winning. As you study this story, imagine yourself on a lake fishing. You have a large trout on your line. It uses every possible trick to get loose from the hook, but with patience and skill you finally land it in your boat. This woman tried repeatedly to rid herself of Jesus, but He countered her every effort until she expressed her faith in Him. Step-by-step He overcame her negative attitudes until He landed her in His boat. And like Jesus, you must never give up on a lost person. The gospel is God's power to save all who believe in His Son.

The Approach (John 4:1-8)

In going from Judea to Galilee or from Galilee to Judea, Jesus usually crossed the Jordan River and traveled through Perea. This was in order to escape the hostility of the Samaritans. John said that Jesus "must needs" go through Samaria (v. 4), or due north from Judea to Galilee. This means that it was a moral and spiritual necessity that He do so. Presently, we learn the reason for it.

Jesus arrived at Jacob's well at "about the sixth hour" or noon (v. 6). The disciples had gone to nearby Sychar to buy food. It was then that the woman arrived to draw water. Due to her unsavory character, she chose this time rather than late afternoon to avoid the other women.

In soul-winning one has to make contact with the lost person. It is best to do so through a common interest. I have known Christian men who played golf or went fishing with a lost man for that very purpose. The only thing Jesus had of common interest with this woman was water. She had come to draw water, and He was thirsty. So He asked, "Give me to drink" (v. 7). Thus began a dialogue or a battle of wits, so to speak.

The Episode (John 4:9-26)

The woman's reply reeked with *scorn*. "How is it that thou, being a Jew, askest drink of me, which am a woman of Samaria?" (v. 9). For the benefit of his Greek readers John added, "For the Jews have no dealings with the Samaritans."

This condition was rooted in the rivalry between the twelve tribes of Israel. Following Solomon's death, ten of the tribes followed Jeroboam I in forming the Northern Kingdom of Israel. Only the tribes of Judah and Benjamin remained loyal to Rehoboam to form the Southern Kingdom of Judah. In 722 B.C. the Northern Kingdom fell to Assyria. The so-called upper class of Israel was taken into captivity, leaving only the lower class in the land. Non-Israelites were brought in to repopulate the land. In time they intermarried with the Israelites to produce the Samaritans.

All of this animosity, plus more, came out in the woman's reply to

Jesus. It would be different to pour more scorn into a sentence than is in the Samaritan woman's reply to Jesus: a Jew and a Samaritan (most likely she pronounced "Jew" with a sneer); a man and a woman; a rabbi (so she thought) and a notorious character (according to one rabbi, a rabbi was not supposed to speak to a woman in public); and religious differences. As they say in baseball, she "touched all the bases" of prejudice: nationality, race, religion, and sex. Implied in all this is the idea that if she gave Jesus a drink from her water pot, His lips would touch where hers had. No Jew would touch his lips to a place where those of a Samaritan's had been.

However, Jesus refused to be sidetracked by any of these. Instead, He said, "If thou knewest the gift of God, and who it is that saith to thee, Give me to drink; thou wouldest have asked of him, and he would have given thee living water" (v. 10).

Here Jesus implied His messiahship. But back of the figures He used was the distinction between *dead* water and *living* water. Dead water was seepage water. Rainwater seeped down through the soil to form a well. The water in Jacob's well was seepage or dead water. *Living* water flowed up out of an artesian spring in a limitless supply. In the Old Testament, Jehovah is pictured as a Fountain of living water (Ps. 36:9; Jer. 2:13; 17:13). Of course, the living water of which Jesus spoke was Himself as Jehovah in flesh.

In the woman's materialistic mind, Jesus' words made no sense. So she sought to insert into the conversation a matter of local pride, Jacob's association with the nearby well (vv. 11-12). But Jesus again refused to be deterred in His purpose.

He reminded the woman of something she knew all too well. If one draws water from Jacob's well, one will become thirsty again. "But whosoever drinketh of the water that I shall give him shall never thirst; but the water that I shall give him shall be in him a well of water springing up into everlasting life" (v. 14). "Never" translates a double negative. In English a double negative makes a positive statement. But in Greek a double negative makes a stronger negative. "Not never thirst" means most certainly one will not thirst again. Of course, Jesus thought of the soul.

But still thinking materialistically, the woman replied, "Sir, give me this water, that I thirst not, neither come hither to draw" (v. 15). Even though she did not grasp the deeper meaning of Jesus' words, at least He got her attention. Anything to avoid thirst and this long daily trip to the well! She thought of creature comfort, but Jesus spoke of soul security.

A professional fund-raiser told me that in his work the easiest thing for which to raise money was a hospital. The hardest thing was raising money for a school. He concluded that people care more for their bodies than they do for their minds. It is also true that we think more of our bodies than we do for our souls.

Let me give you a simple test. Before attending church, on which do you spend the most time: beautifying and clothing your body or preparing your soul for worship? I fear that most of us, if not all, would fail that test.

At this point Jesus saw that He was making no progress in His effort to lead the woman to think about spiritual things. So He used the shock treatment on her. Like a skilled physician, He put His finger on the sorest spot in her life. He said, "Go, call thy husband, and come hither" (v. 16). As some would say, He quit preaching and started meddling. What He did was to lance the boil of sin in her personal life.

Let us suppose that you walked into a surgical room in a hospital, not knowing where you were. You see a group of men and women standing about a table. Each one is wearing strange robes and small masks as if to conceal his or her identity. You see an unconscious man strapped to the table. A large incision has been made in his chest. Standing over him is a man with what appears to be a knife in his hand. You gasp as you think, *My soul, they are performing what appears to be a ritual murder!* Actually, a dedicated and skilled surgeon is performing a heart bypass in an effort to save the man's life.

In Hebrews 4:12-13, the author described the Word of God as a sword that cuts into soul and spirit. The Word of God judges even "the thoughts and intents of the heart." "Neither is there any creature that is not manifest in his sight." So it was that Jesus, the living Word of God, opened up this woman's life, that she along with Him might see the sordid nature of her life. He did it, not to hurt or destroy her. He did so in an effort to save her soul.

Jesus told her that she spoke the truth when she said that she had no husband, "For thou hast had five husbands; and he whom thou now hast is not thy husband" (v. 18). She had gone from husband to husband, and she was at the time living with a man out of wedlock. It sounds rather modern, does it not?

At this point Jesus gained her *respect*. For she said, "Sir, I perceive that thou art a prophet" (v. 19). Though Jesus was a stranger to her, He knew about her life-style. We can be sure that He knows ours!

But she changed the subject. The most difficult words to utter in any language are "I have sinned." So rather than to admit it, the woman sought to shift the conversation to an argument about religious differences between Jews and Samaritans.

I heard of a pastor trying to lead a lost man to Christ. Finally, the man said, "Preacher, I will become a Christian if you will tell me who was Cain's wife." As if that had anything to do with becoming a Christian! The pastor replied, "She was Mrs. Cain. Now let us get back on our subject."

The woman dug up the old argument between Jews and Samaritans as to the proper place to worship, Mount Moriah in Jerusalem or Mount Gerizim in Samaria (v. 20). When the woman said "this mountain," she probably pointed to nearby Mount Gerizim. As you stand at Jacob's well, Mount Gerizim and Mount Ebal tower above it, with a narrow valley in between them.

In an effort to justify their claim to be the true people of God, the Samaritans rewrote what is known as the Samaritan Pentateuch (Genesis—Deuteronomy). For instance, it read that Abraham's near sacrifice of Isaac took place on Mount Gerizim rather than on Mount Moriah in what is now Jerusalem. Sanballat even built a temple on Mount Gerizim to rival the one in Jerusalem, but it was destroyed by John Hyrcanus of Jerusalem in 129 B.C. In recent years its ruins have been excavated. Even to this day, the Samaritans hold certain services there, such as the feast of Passover.

Seldom if ever is a person led to Christ through debate. Not to be caught in that booby trap, Jesus brushed the problem aside.

"Woman, believe me, the hour cometh, when ye shall neither in this mountain, nor yet in Jerusalem, worship the Father" (v. 21). The temple of Mount Gerizim was gone. In A.D. 70, the one in Jerusalem would be destroyed.

However, the main emphasis of Jesus was not on the *place* but on the spirit of true worship. For "God is a Spirit: and they that worship him must worship him in spirit and in truth" (v. 24). Going to church does not necessarily mean that you worship.

Thwarted in her effort to lure Jesus into religious debate, the woman said, "I know that Messias cometh, which is called Christ: when he is come, he will tell us all things" (v. 25). He will clear up this difference in religion.

Since among the Jews the term *Messiah* or "Christ" had a military-political connotation, Jesus avoided its use. He commended Peter for his confession (Matt. 16:16-17). Testifying under oath before the Sanhedrin, Jesus admitted that He was the Christ (Matt. 26:63-64). Otherwise, He would have committed perjury. And in this private conversation, He said plainly that He was the Messiah. He did so to bring this woman face-to-face in her decision concerning Him. She had failed to shake off the hook. So now Jesus brought her into His boat. He brought her to faith in Himself.

Sooner or later, you must make a personal decision concerning Christ. You cannot avoid Him. To postpone a decision is to deny Him. Either you receive Him or you reject Him. This is your hour of decision. What will you do then with Jesus who is called Christ (Matt. 27:22)?

The Woman's Faith in Jesus (John 4:27-30,39-42)

Her faith made her a *witness*. In her haste to share her faith with others, she left her water pot and rushed into Sychar. Various ideas have been offered as to why she left her water pot behind: excitement made her forget it, she could run faster without it, and having drunk living water the pot no longer mattered. I like William Barclay's suggestion. She left the pot at the well because she knew that she would return to where Jesus was. But, first, she must share the good news.

Arriving in Sychar she said to some men, "Come, see a man, which told me all things that ever I did: is not this the Christ?" (v. 29). In the Greek, her question calls for a negative answer. We would say, "This is not the Christ, is it?"

Why did she give this negative witness? These men knew her life. Apparently she feared that they would laugh at her. But it was a witness, and God honored it, for it had its desired effect. The verb tense of "went out" means that immediately they went to see Jesus for themselves. They too believed in Him (v. 41). To the woman they said, "Now we believe, not because of thy saying: for we have heard him ourselves, and know that this is indeed the Christ, the Saviour of the world" (v. 42)—not Savior of Jews only, or Samaritans only, but of the whole world. Had it not been for this woman's witness, they would not have heard Jesus at all!

Now let us review the stages through which the Samaritan woman passed under the skillful guidance of Jesus: from *scorn* to *attention*, to *respect*, to *faith*, to *witnessing*. You do not scorn Jesus, but are you ignoring Him? What He can do for you should command your attention. He is worthy of your respect. And He will prove trustworthy if you believe in Him as your Savior. Will you do so right now? And having trusted in Him, you should be a witness to others of your faith in and experience with Jesus. Only thus has God ordained that the gospel will be heard. Only thus may Jesus become in reality what He is in divine intent—the Savior of the world.

4
What a Difference a Day Makes!

(John 5)

"Immediately the man was made whole, and took up his bed, and walked: and on the same day was the sabbath" (John 5:9).

For the title of this sermon I am indebted to a song that was popular when I was a young man. It was a song sung by a lover to his beloved. Its setting was a happy one.

I invite you to join me as we consider it in an unhappy environment. It involves a good work that Jesus did on the Sabbath Day and the unhappy consequences that followed. Thus we will see the other side of "What a Difference a Day Makes." For the Jewish leaders placed the institution of the Sabbath above human need. They valued their sacred day more than they valued a lame person. They abused rather than used this day as God intended.

We also abuse rather than use the Lord's Day as God wills. The purpose of this sermon is to teach us how we should use this day for the glory of God.

The Healing of a Lame Man (John 5:1-9a)

Jesus was in Jerusalem attending "a feast of the Jews," probably a Passover (John 5:1). In the city there was a pool called Bethesda, house of mercy. It was located near "the place of the sheep" or sheep gate. It had "five porches" or colonnaded areas (v. 2). Since its waters moved periodically, it probably was fed by an underground spring that flowed intermittently (verse 4 is not in the best texts), something like Old Faithful in Yellowstone National Park. The Jews believed that when the water stirred, the first person to get into the pool would be healed. Therefore, the place was crowded with the sick, lame, and blind.

For years, some scholars denied that such a pool existed. They held that John's Gospel was written in the second century by an Elder John from Ephesus. According to them he had only a tourist's knowledge of Palestine, that the Gospel was only a theological treatise, and that its historical references were not to be trusted.

However, in recent years this site has been excavated by archaeologists. They found the pool exactly where John says that it was. And it has the foundations for five colonnaded areas, one on each of the four sides and one down the middle. This shows that rather than a tourist's knowledge, the author was familiar with the topography of Jerusalem prior to its destruction by the Romans in A.D. 70. Also, it strengthens the traditional authorship by the apostle John and a date probably A.D. 80-90.

Among those about the pool was a man who had been lame for thirty-eight years. He was probably brought there daily by his family or by friends. Yet in spite of this he was still lame. Jesus asked him, "Wilt thou be made whole?" (v. 6). Of course, he wanted to be healed. That was why he was there. Jesus' question was designed to get his attention.

The man responded by explaining that due to his condition, with no one to help him, someone else always got into the pool ahead of him (v. 7). Notice that Jesus did not offer to help him at the next stirring of the waters. He was not taken in by this superstition. Instead, He told the man immediately to "rise, take up thy bed [pallet], and walk" (v. 8). Literally the phrase means, "Immediately rise, and immediately take up your pallet, and go on walking about." This picture comes out in the verb tenses. The same is true in verse 9. The healing and taking up of his pallet were immediate acts. "Walk" expresses the healed man's progress as he went on walking about.

If the man had refused to obey Jesus' words, he would have remained a cripple. When he obeyed Him, he found strength in his leg muscles that enabled him to do as Jesus said. His was no gradual healing. It was a miracle. In fact, this is one of seven "signs" or miracles about which John built his Gospel. It was no mere psychological reaction in the man's mind. It was a miracle of strength in his feet and legs.

Some people deny miracles as being contrary to natural law. Perhaps we need a working definition of miracle. A miracle is an act of God, contrary to natural law as human beings understand it but not contrary to natural law as God understands it, and which He performs in accord with His benevolent will and redemptive purpose.

Humanity knows *some* of God's natural laws, but not *all* of them. It has been my privilege to live during the greatest period of change in the history of the world. Things that are regarded as commonplace today would have been called miracles when I was born. Examples of this are practically endless. Take, for example, the fields of electronics, medicine, and travel.

In the late 1880s, the head of the patent office in Washington resigned. He felt there was no future in his job. He said that everything that could be invented had been invented. How silly these words sound today! He stood on the threshold of history's greatest period of invention, and he did not know it.

We speak of *research*, but perhaps we should speak of *revelation*. Laws known to God from the beginning He reveals to us as He chooses. Who can say what laws of higher dimension still are known to God and of which we, as yet, are ignorant?

I am not denying the miracle. To the contrary, I am pointing out that there is no logical ground on which to question it. If human beings can do what they have done, who is to question what God can do? Once we fully accept the opening words of the Bible—"In the beginning God"—all else in the Bible comes easy. Instead of questioning Jesus' power to heal this man, knowing Him, we would have been surprised if He had not healed him.

The Problem of the Sabbath (John 5:9b-18)

John 5:9 closes thus: "on the same day was the sabbath." This was no afterthought on John's part. Rather it is the heart of the story.

"The Jews" (v. 10) is used by John to refer to Jesus' opponents. This man, with his pallet on his shoulder, was joyfully walking about—probably in the temple area. Some members of the Sanhedrin, probably Pharisees, accosted him. They said, "It is the sabbath day: it is not lawful for thee to carry thy bed" (v. 10). By whose law? Certainly the Fourth Commandment made no such fine distinction (Ex. 20:8-10). The law they referred to was one of hundreds of rules laid down by the rabbis as to what one could or could not do on the Sabbath. One law said that people could not bear a burden on that day. A burden was defined as anything weighing more than two figs.

The Jews did not deny that a miracle had taken place. Perhaps the lame man was a familiar figure. Now he was walking about, bearing the pallet which for so long had borne him. The problem was that he had been healed and was bearing his pallet on the Sabbath Day. None of these Jews congratulated the man on being healed. Apparently that was not important to them. Their tremendous problem was the preservation of their sacred day.

In order to understand this, we must consider the place of the Sabbath in Judaism. Like the Jews, other religions had their temples, scriptures, and traditions. Only Judaism had the Sabbath. So they were especially sensitive at that point.

A multitude of rules had been compiled to regulate life on the Sabbath Day. For instance, a Sabbath Day's journey was limited to a little less than three-fourths of a mile. But the rabbis defined one's home as where one had shelter and took meals. So if a rabbi planned to take a trip of five miles on the Sabbath, he arranged beforehand to have little brush arbors built at intervals along the way, with a piece of bread and a small portion of wine at each place. Then on the Sabbath he would travel the allowed distance, sit under the arbor, take a bite of bread, and a drink of wine. Then he would go to the next arbor, and so on to the end of his journey.

Also the rabbis debated whether or not one should eat an egg laid on the Sabbath because the hen worked. Dragging a stick on the ground on that day was forbidden—that was plowing. A woman was not to look into a mirror on the Sabbath lest she see a gray hair and pull it out; that was shearing. Debates were held on many puzzling questions. For instance, suppose a man were riding home at sunset on Friday, the beginning of the Sabbath. Should he remove the saddle from his donkey? That constituted work. Should he leave the saddle on the donkey? Then the donkey worked. Should a man with a sore throat gargle with oil? It was agreed that this was forbidden. But he could drink oil as food. If in the process it helped his throat, that was purely incidental. Jesus never violated the Fourth Commandment, but it is understandable that He ignored such silly rules.

However, John had a purpose in noting that Jesus healed a lame man on the Sabbath Day. The Jewish leaders had opposed Jesus from the beginning (John 2:18-21). Having no particular issue, they opposed Him on general principles. But now they had an issue—Jesus' ignoring their Sabbath rules—and they played it to the hilt. "Therefore did the Jews persecute Jesus, and sought to slay him, because he had done these things on the sabbath day" (v. 16).

When they faced Jesus with the matter, He justified His act by saying, "My Father worketh hitherto, and I work" (v. 17). Literally He said, "My Father keeps on working, and I keep on working." "Sabbath" means "rest." The Sabbath Day commemorated God's rest from creating. He did not rest because He was tired but because He had finished His creative work. And He continues to work in providential care and redemption. He does not cease from either of these on the Sabbath Day.

Like the Father, Jesus the Son keeps on doing His work regardless of the day. Literally, Jesus said, "I myself [like the Father] keep on working." In fact, in John 5:19-38 Jesus showed that He is so identified with the Father that the work of One is the work of the other.

So the Jews sought all the more to kill Jesus not only because He healed on the Sabbath but because He made Himself "equal with God" (v. 18). The charge was true, of course, but not as these Jews intended. Jesus not only was equal with God, He was God Himself in flesh doing the works of God.

The truth is that in their observance of the Sabbath, the Jews had practically made it a substitute for God. As seen in the case at hand, they wanted to make God Himself inoperative on that day. Viewing their attitude toward the Sabbath, we find ourselves in sympathy with the little boy in the following story.

On Sunday the boy was made to dress up for attending Sunday School and church service. He was uncomfortable in his Sunday-go-to-meeting clothes. Arriving back home he put on his shirt and overalls. Happy as a bird released from its cage, the boy whistled as he hopped and skipped through the house. In a stern voice the father said, "Son, stop whistling. This is the Lord's Day!" Crestfallen, the boy wandered out to the barn lot. There he saw the family mule. Its head was down, its eyes were half-closed, its ears were flopped down, and its lower lip sagged. As J. D. Grey was fond of saying, "Its head was long enough to eat ice cream out of a churn." Seeing this spectacle, the boy put his arms around the mule's head and said, "Poor old mule! You must belong to Daddy's church too!"

If the Jews erred in one direction concerning the Sabbath, many today do the same in the opposite direction. We need a balance between the two.

The Lord of the Sabbath

It was on another Sabbath Day that Jesus and His disciples were returning to Galilee following the visit to Jerusalem recorded in John 5 (see Matt. 12:1-8; Mark 2:23-28; Luke 6:1-5). They were passing through a grain field that was beginning to ripen. Farmers left paths in their fields over which travelers passed. The disciples were hungry, so they were plucking heads of grain, rubbing away the chaff, and eating the grain. According to Deuteronomy 23:25 this was permissible so long as they did not use a sickle to cut the grain (Matt. 12:1).

They were accompanied by some Pharisees who apparently had been sent to spy on Jesus. Seeing what the disciples were doing, they said to Jesus, "Behold, thy disciples do that which is not lawful to do upon the sabbath day" (v. 2). Any other day of the week it would have been lawful, but not on the Sabbath.

This is another example of their rigid rules governing observance of the Sabbath. The rabbis defined plucking heads of grain as reaping, rubbing them in their hands as threshing, and blowing away the chaff was winnowing. The entire process involved preparation of food.

In Haifa, Israel, Frances and I went to the dining room one morning for an early breakfast. Our party had paid extra in order to have an American breakfast, such as bacon and eggs. Upon entering the dining room we found a buffet table filled with cold food such as fish, boiled eggs, and the like. I reminded the waiter of the special arrangement for our party. But he said that it was impossible. Somewhat put out, I asked why. He said, "It is the Sabbath." We had forgotten that it was Saturday. Hearing that, this Baptist preacher and his wife meekly ate a cold breakfast.

In reply to the Jews, Jesus cited two Old Testament passages. He reminded the Pharisees of the event when David and his men ate the shewbread in the tabernacle, bread that by law was eventually to be eaten by the priests (1 Sam. 21:6). Also He recalled how the priests worked on the Sabbath in connection with worship (Num. 28:9-10). Too, He quoted Hosea 6:6, "I desired mercy, and not sacrifice." In each case He justified the action of His disciples. In 12:11-12, Matthew related that on the following Sabbath in the synagogue in Capernaum, Jesus healed a man with a withered hand. Before He did it, the Pharisees asked if it was lawful "to heal on the sabbath days? that they might accuse him" (12:10). In reply, He asked them a question, "What man shall there be among you, that shall have one sheep, and if it fall into a pit on the sabbath day, will he not lay hold on it, and lift it out? How much then is a man better than a sheep? Wherefore it is lawful to do well on the sabbath days" (vv. 11-12).

Looking back at Matthew 12:8, Jesus said, "For the Son of man is Lord even of the sabbath day." Not the Pharisees, the rabbis, or the Sanhedrin were Lord of the Sabbath. Incidentally, since Jesus is Jehovah in flesh, one may see in this claim the idea that the Son as God gave the Fourth Commandment in the first place. In any case, He made clear the divine intent for this Commandment.

By way of summary, in word and example Jesus taught three

classes of acts are permissible on the Sabbath: deeds of necessity, deeds of worship, and deeds of mercy. Any deed that fits any one of these categories has Jesus' approval on the Sabbath Day.

One thing more needs to be said at this point. According to Mark 2:27, just before declaring Himself as Lord of the Sabbath, Jesus said, "The sabbath was made for man, and not man for the sabbath."

The Jewish religious leaders said that people were made to keep the Sabbath. To them, the person did not count; they made the *institution* more important than the person. We have seen this in every cited incident. On the other hand, God made the Sabbath for humanity. What God had given to be a blessing, they had made a blight and a burden. But let it be hastily added, this is no scriptural ground for a wide-open Sunday! Such is as great an abuse of the divine intent as the practice of the Jews in Jesus' day.

Does someone ask, "What does the Jewish Sabbath have to do with me? I am a Christian!" Well, for one thing, what the Bible says about keeping the Sabbath applies to the day set apart for Christian worship. We have noted that "sabbath" means "rest." It has nothing to do with the number of the day. The Old Testament Sabbath commemorated God's rest after He had finished His creative work. In the New Testament, the Christians observed "the first day of the week" to celebrate our Lord's resurrection, or the finish of God's work of redemption. The word *Sunday* is not a New Testament word. It just happens to be the first day of the Roman calendar week. One time it is called the "Lord's Day" (Rev. 1:10). Pagans observed the first day of each month as Emperor's Day. In defiance of emperor worship, Christians called the first day of the week the Lord's Day. In the New Testament, the day on which Christians as such joined in public worship is always the first day of the week (Acts 20:7; 1 Cor. 16:2).

Like the Sabbath, this day was made for humanity. We need one day out of seven in which to recuperate both physically and spiritually.

Many years ago I read about an experiment made by a railroad company. They purchased two locomotives that were exactly alike. One was used constantly, week after week and year after year. The boiler fires were never extinguished. The other was used six days each week. Then the boiler fires were extinguished. It was allowed to rest on the seventh day. The metal cooled and/or reset itself. It was found that the latter locomotive lasted longer and needed less maintenance than the former.

If metal needs to rest one day out of seven, surely the delicate nature of the human body needs the same. But in our worldly lifestyle the weekends, including the Lord's Day, have made that day a holiday instead of a holy day. So we return to work on Blue Monday in worse shape than we were on Friday. It is no wonder that we live in a pressure-cooker atmosphere. Our bodies pay such a toll, to say nothing about our starved souls. We cannot violate God's laws without paying the price for such.

Some years ago, we spent a weekend in Moscow. Our sole purpose for going was to attend the Moscow Baptist Church. Since we were leaving the next day, after the service the ladies wanted to buy some souvenirs of Russia. Our guide said, "We can windowshop. But you will have to wait until tomorrow to buy something. The stores are closed today." When asked why, she replied, "Because it is Sunday."

Here is a nation that officially does not recognize that God exists. Its sole purpose is to build a strong nation. Yet it recognizes that the human body needs one day out of seven for rest. I was tempted to ask our guide to send some missionaries to our so-called Christian nation to teach us how to observe the Lord's Day.

5
Turning Your Back upon Jesus

(John 6:1-69)

"From that time many of his disciples went back, and walked no more with him" (John 6:66).

One of our most beautiful invitation hymns calls us to turn our eyes upon Jesus, but, strangely, for many the opposite is true. Instead of turning their eyes upon Jesus in faith, they turn their backs upon Him in rejection. We see such in John 6.

One of John's purposes in writing his Gospel was to supplement the accounts of the other three that preceded his. Even where John paralleled them, he gave details not contained in them. Other than beginning with the final week leading up to Jesus's crucifixion and resurrection, the only place where John paralleled the other Gospels is the feeding of the five thousand. He did this to show the reason for the collapse of Jesus' Galilean ministry. For instance, following the miraculous feeding, the people tried to make Jesus a king or a political-military Messiah. Of course, He refused the role.

Though frustrated by this refusal, nevertheless, the same crowd came to Jesus the next morning at the synagogue in Capernaum. It is at this point that we pick up the account. The purpose of this message is to show why people, having heard the truth, turn their backs upon Him who is Truth.

The Materialistic Crowd (John 6:24-34)

Up to this point in His Galilean ministry, Jesus could not escape the crowds. Even when He crossed the sea of Galilee, they came to

Him. It was then that He fed the multitude. The next day they sought Him again in Capernaum.

With His solemn "Verily, verily" Jesus said, "Ye seek me, not because ye saw the miracles [signs], but because ye did eat of the loaves, and were filled" (v. 26).

"See" means "to see with perception." With their natural eyes they saw the loaves, but they did not perceive the meaning behind the sign. The feeding of the multitude was the fourth sign about which John built his Gospel. These were signs denoting Jesus' deity. But in their materialistic minds they failed to see the true nature of Jesus. All they did was to eat the food, and they were filled.

"Were filled" renders a verb used in nonbiblical Greek for a cow receiving food. She did not thank the giver or ask for what purpose it was given. She merely ate it and filled her stomach. These people were like the cow. The message of the sign failed to penetrate their understanding. They thought only of their material needs. They sought Jesus now only because they were hungry again.

The story is told of a farmer who visited a large city. In a restaurant he ordered food and prayed a prayer of thanks before eating it. At the next table sat some tough young men. One cried, "Hey, Rube! Where you come from, does everyone pray before eating?" The farmer replied, "Everyone except the hogs."

So many people take for granted the blessings of life. Blessings are but a means of satisfying their creature needs. They never stop to realize that God is the giver of every good and perfect gift. They think the world owes them a living. So they never look beyond the material to its spiritual significance. They live only at the animal level. As the result, they have fat bodies and famished souls.

Yet Jesus sought to lead those people beyond the physical to their spiritual needs (v. 27). They needed to look beyond perishable food to that which produces eternal life. He had given them the loaves and fishes only a few hours before this. And now they were hungry again. But if they had only believed in Him, He would have given them food which endures in eternal life.

True to their Jewish belief, they asked what they must do in order to work the works of God (v. 28). Jesus' answer was to "believe on him [Jesus] whom he [God] hath sent" (v. 29). In other words, it was not a salvation through works; it was by God's grace through faith. Too many people think of works instead of grace.

No matter how many good works you may do, they cannot merit one second of the life Jesus offers to all believers in Him. It is ever "Nothing in my hand I bring / Simply to thy cross I cling."[1]

The crowd's response would be humorous were it not so serious. Ignoring the miracle of the day before, to say nothing about previous healing miracles (John 6:2), they demanded that Jesus show them a sign to prove that He could give them more food as He promised. Through Moses, God had given their fathers daily manna. Implied is the fact that yesterday's food was gone. Now they wanted more. They were still thinking at the animal level (vv. 30-31). With His "Verily, verily" Jesus replied by contrasting perishable manna with the true bread that God gives (v. 32). "For the bread of God·is he which cometh down from heaven, and giveth life unto the world" (v. 33).

In turn, still thinking at the animal level, they said, "Lord, evermore give us this bread" (v. 34). Like the Samaritan woman, they were eager to receive physical bread that would prevent hunger forever.

The attitude expressed in the people's request for a sign brings to mind the story of two men. One spoke unkindly of a third man. The other expressed surprise, reminding the man that the third man had done his critic many favors. "Yes," he replied, "but he hasn't done anything lately." Had someone reminded the crowd of the event on the previous day, they probably would have said, "Oh, that was yesterday! But this is a new day." How soon we forget blessings of God!

Every day I receive junk mail urging me to send back the enclosed card. The promise is that by doing so I may win millions of dollars. I have never returned one, placing the whole thing in File 13. But apparently many do. It is an expression of animal greed. Yet how few of these would not hedge if you offered them eternal spiritual riches through faith in Jesus Christ? It is because so many live at the level of materialism.

The Bread from Heaven (John 6:35-65)

The crowd wanted the bread of God that comes down from heaven and gives life to the world (vv. 33-34). In a sense Jesus said, "You have it!" "I am the bread of life: he that cometh to me shall never hunger; and he that believeth on me shall never thirst" (v. 35). "I" is emphatic, so "I myself" or "I and no one else." Both uses of "never" translate a strong double negative. Most assuredly those who believe in Jesus will never hunger or thirst. "Hunger" and "thirst" represent the two basic things necessary for physical life. Thus Jesus said that faith in Him as Savior is absolutely necessary for eternal life. These people had seen Him, yet they did not believe in Him (v. 36).

The words "All that the Father giveth me shall come to me; . . . And . . . all which he hath given me" (vv. 37,39) are interpreted by some to mean that God has chosen certain people to the neglect of all others. However, the overall teachings of the Bible say that God wills to save as many, not as few, as possible. However, it is more in keeping with the biblical context to see God's purpose to save all who believe in Jesus. "All" means "every single one of the whole." Actually, God has taken the initiative in salvation. He is seeking humanity, not humanity seeking God. This is the difference between Christianity and all other religions. God in Christ has provided salvation for all people. But it becomes a reality in each person as he or she receives Jesus as Savior. Consequently, the final result rests with you. As one made in God's image you are a spiritual person endowed with the right of choice, but God holds you responsible for the choices you make.

Some say that they do not believe a God of love would create a soul and then send it to hell. God is love (1 John 4:8). But He is also holiness, righteousness, and truth. As God, He cannot violate His nature. He is fatherly in His nature and longs to be the Father of all people. But He is Father in truth only to those who have become His children through faith in His Son. If you go to hell, it is because you yourself choose to do so. God has done all even He can do to save you from hell. But you must receive His redemptive work through your personal faith in Jesus Christ.

Those who come to Christ, He will "in no wise cast out" (v. 37). "In no wise cast out" is the strongest statement possible in this regard. It contains the strong double negative "no wise." "Cast out" is the verb "to cast" with the prefix "out." And for good measure it ends with the word for "outside." The *New English Bible* reads, "I will never turn away." *The New Berkeley Version* says, "I will certainly not cast out." But neither of these is as strong as the Greek text. Literally translated, it reads, "Me not never I cast out outside." It is impossible fully to translate it into smooth English.

Someone said that a little knowledge is a dangerous thing. This truth is borne out here. These Galileans knew just enough about Jesus to provide a stumbling block to their faith.

"The Jews then murmured at him, because he said, I am the bread which came down from heaven" (v. 41). The Greek word for "murmured," when pronounced, has in it the sound of the buzzing of angry bees. In a sense they said, "We know Him and His family. So He can't be much" (see v. 42). They knew nothing about Jesus' virgin birth. Insofar as they were concerned, Joseph, now dead, had been His father. In fact, Joseph was His foster father. In any case, how could this former carpenter of Nazareth be Bread that "came down from heaven" (v. 42)?

Instead of backing off, Jesus pressed forward. He claimed that He alone had seen the Father (v. 46). Calling again for faith in Him, He insisted that He is the "bread of life." Unlike manna whose consumers were dead, He is living Bread. Those eating this Bread will live forever (vv. 47-51). In verse 51 to "bread" Jesus added His "flesh." This contains a hint to the effect that in the wilderness the Israelites had eaten both manna and quail.

Hearing this, the Jews "strove among themselves, saying, How can this man give us his flesh to eat?" (v. 52). "Strove" carries the idea of a civil war within their ranks. In their materialistic outlook, they cold think of flesh only as meat. But Jesus continued to press the idea, adding the drinking of His blood (vv. 53-58).

Of course, Jesus was thinking of the close relationship between Himself and those believing in Him. We take into our bodies various types of food. Through the processes of digestion and assimilation these various foods become parts of our bodies. We become so related that these things become ourselves.

So it is when we through faith partake of Christ. By the power of the Holy Spirit, we become the very parts of Jesus' body, the body of Christ. In 1 Corinthians 12, Paul dealt with this at length and in detail. As God is incarnated in Christ, so is He incarnated in us, and we in Him. All this is expressed in the word *fellowship*. A mystery? Yes. And one must experience it in faith to understand it. We cannot *explain* it in words. But we can *experience* it in the Holy Spirit.

The Mass Desertion and the Faithful Few (John 6:66-69)

After Jesus finished, the people said, "This is an hard saying; who can hear it?" (v. 60). In their materialistic mind-set, they failed to see the true meaning of Jesus' words. To them a literal interpretation of eating Jesus' flesh and drinking His blood sounded like cannibalism. Despite Jesus' reminder that He had spoken in spiritual—not literal—terms, the crowd turned its back on Him and walked away. "From that time many of his disciples went back, and walked no more with him" (v. 66).

Jesus' followers were called disciples. But the Greek word so translated means "learners." In each case, the context must decide the true meaning of the word. Here it does not mean Christians who rejected Jesus and thus lost their salvation. These were simply learners who had not received Him as Savior (v. 64a). They had followed Jesus to see His miracles, but they had not accepted His words or even understood the purpose of His miracles. Like so many people today, they accepted only that which they could experience through their natural senses.

The day before, they tried forcibly to make Jesus a political-military messiah. But He refused the role. They even would have accepted Him as a bread messiah. But that Jesus refused to be. When it became clear to them as to His spiritual mission, they wanted none of it. In other words, when Jesus refused to be the kind of messiah they wanted, they, in turn, refused Him as the Messiah He willed to be.

A man refused to become a Christian because he did not like a bloody religion. But God sets the terms of our redemption. For "without shedding of blood [there] is no remission of sins (Heb. 9:22).

As with the rich young ruler, so here, Jesus' heart ached to see the departing throngs. Never after this do we see Galilean crowds following Jesus. Luke (9:51—18:37) records crowds following Him in Judea—but nevermore in Galilee. Did Jesus fail in Galilee in His eighteen-month ministry? No. He faithfully proclaimed God's Word. The people of Galilee failed because they, for the most part, rejected Him.

Jesus never told His people to be successful but to be faithful. I have had people say they do not witness for Christ for fear that they would fail to lead people to Christ. This was the attitude that a certain farmer had. A passerby noted that his fields were bare. The farmer said, "Well, two years ago the drought ruined my crop. Last year the boll weevils and other insects ruined it. So I decided to play it safe this year. I did not plant anything."

If we witness for Christ, we cannot fail. In our witnessing we succeed. We are not the judge, jury, or prosecuting attorney. We are the witnesses on the stand. We just tell lost people what the Lord has done for us, love them, and pray for them. Having done these things, the result is between the lost person and the Lord.

Apparently, the departing multitude was a test of the apostles' faith. Perhaps they were getting restless. It is a simple matter to be one of a crowd following Jesus. The true test comes when one is in the minority or stands alone.

So Jesus asked them, "Will ye also go away?" (v. 67). Literally He was asking, "Not also you are willing to go away?" "You" is emphatic, contrasting the twelve with the departing people.

Simon Peter was ever ready with an answer, and we may well imagine that Jesus waited with bated breath to hear the answer. So Peter said, "Lord, to whom shall we go? thou hast the words of eternal life. And we believe and are sure that thou art that Christ, the

Son of the living God" (vv. 68-69). Some strong manuscripts read simply "the holy one of God." In either case, the meaning is the same.

Peter spoke for all except Judas (vv. 70-71); he kept quiet. It is possible that the twelve had weighed the matter. They were like any Christians who are tempted to follow the crowd instead of standing true to their Christian convictions. But they concluded that only Jesus said the words of life.

Then came the confession. In spite of everything, they remained true. They did not understand the depths of the meaning of Jesus' words. But they had a steadfast conviction. The verb tenses "believe" and "are sure" express completion. And "we" and "thou" are emphatic. Literally the disciples said, "We in contrast to the departing crowd have believed, still believe, and will continue to believe, and we know without a shadow of doubt, that you alone are the holy one of God"—God's Chosen, God's Anointed, God's Messiah.

Ah, the faithful few! They are in every Christian fellowship in every church. And in them lie the hope and assurance for the Lord's work!

But still the question remains: "To whom shall we go?" Christian, to whom will you give the first loyalty—to the milling throngs? Or to Christ, who is the same yesterday, today, and forever? Will it be a saved soul and a fruitless Christian life? Or a saved soul and a fruitful life for Christ? Lost person, to whom will you go? To Satan, a wasted life, and an eternity in hell? Or to Christ, a saved soul, useful life, and eternal bliss with Christ in heaven? The choice is yours to make. And in your choice lies eternal consequences.

1. Augustus M. Toplady, "Rock of Ages, Cleft for Me," *Baptist Hymnal* (Nashville: Broadman Press, 1975), No. 163.

6
Confounding the Scholars

(John 9)

"They answered and said unto him, Thou was altogether born in sins, and dost thou teach us? And they cast him out"(John 9:34).

The late Robert G. Lee was fond of saying, "I had rather be a fool on fire than a scholar on ice." He was speaking of being a fool for Christ instead of a so-called scholar who had no faith in Christ.

We have an ideal example of both in John 9. A man who had had a definite experience with Christ opposed the Jewish scholars who were sworn enemies of Christ. The thought before us is that cold, hostile logic cannot prevail against a personal experience with Jesus Christ.

The Healing of a Blind Man (John 9:1-7)

It happened in Jerusalem shortly after the Feast of Tabernacles in early fall of A.D. 29. Jesus and the apostles saw a man who had been blind from birth. He was a beggar (9:8). Evidently they were entering the temple area, a favorite place for beggars (Acts 3:2). People on their way to worship were more likely to be generous.

Seeing him, the apostles asked Jesus, "Master [Rabbi], who did sin, this man, or his parents, that he was born blind?" (v. 2). The ancient Jews believed in prenatal sin. It is possible that the man was born blind because of the sin of his parents. But, of course, the idea of prenatal sin is ridiculous.

Jesus replied, "Neither hath this man sinned, nor his parents: but that the works of God should be made manifest in him. I must work the works of him that sent me, while it is day: the night cometh, when no man can work" (vv. 3-5).

For years these verses bothered me. The way the KJV text reads sounds as if God arbitrarily made this man blind from birth so He could get glory from it. This did not correspond with the revelation of God in the Bible.

One day it dawned on me that the problem lay in the punctuation. The original Greek had no punctuation except the question mark made like our semicolon. The translators punctuated it as they understood it. And since their punctuation was not inspired, I had the right to punctuate it as I understood the passage. The result was as follows: "Neither hath this man sinned, nor his parents [period]. But that the works of God should be made manifest in him, I must work the works of him that sent me, while it is day: the night cometh when no man can work."

It was a matter of satisfaction to me when later I found that the great expositor G. Campbell Morgan punctuated the verses as I did. It expresses divine truth in keeping with the nature of God.

When the apostles saw the blind man, they wanted to appoint a committee to determine the cause and who was to blame. Jesus brushed both views aside as being untrue. In effect, He said, "The fact is that the man is blind. So what are we going to do about it? I must restore his sight while I have the opportunity." God was glorified, but that was because Jesus healed the man from blindness.

It is often said that a camel looks like something put together by a committee. I have also heard that the best committee is composed of three people: one is sick, and one is out of town.

Too often we want to appoint a committee to study a matter when we already know what to do. I am not opposed to committees. If I had a dollar for every hour I have spent serving on denominational committees, I could retire in luxury. But we should never make a committee a substitute for known duty.

Jesus used spittle and dirt to make mud which He put on the man's eyes. Since Jesus healed other blind people without this, we may assume that this was done to strengthen the man's faith. Then

Jesus told him to wash in the pool of Siloam. He did and "came seeing" (v. 7). Again, this was on the Sabbath Day (v. 14).

The Resultant Dilemma (John 9:8-23)

The healing of this man caused quite a stir. Apparently he was well known by his neighbors. When he returned to his neighborhood, people began to ask questions. Was this the blind beggar to whom they had given coins all these years? If so, had he been pretending to be blind? Some said he was the one. Others said he looked like him. Restored eyesight had changed his appearance. But the man ended all questions by saying, "I am he" (v. 9).

Then their questions shifted to the identity of the one who had healed him (vv. 11-12). After the man explained that one called Jesus had done it and how it had taken place, they wanted to know His whereabouts, but the healed man did not know (vv. 11-12). As in the case of the lame man (John 5), Jesus had slipped away. He knew what would happen when the man was discovered having his eyesight. He did not perform this miracle for personal acclaim; He did it because the man was in need of help. He did not want to be known merely as a miracle worker.

Instead of rejoicing that the man was healed or trying to find Jesus, they carted the healed man off to the Pharisees. Why the Pharisees? Because Jesus had healed on the Sabbath Day. Again John slipped this little item into his account. He did it for a purpose. Most likely the people took the man to the Pharisees out of fear that they might get into trouble if, knowing this, they did not report it (see v. 22).

In response to the Pharisees' questions, the man again told how he was healed (v. 15). The rejoinder of some of the Pharisees was, "This man is not of God, because he keepeth not the sabbath day" (v. 16). Others questioned that decision: "How can a man that is a sinner do such miracles?"

Over against the baseless blanket accusations of some was the obvious fact that Jesus worked miracles. So there was a division or schism among the theologians. At least, some of them were not so blinded by prejudice as to refuse to recognize the evidence before their very eyes. But, alas, there are still some philosophers pretending to be theologians who deny the deity of Jesus in spite of the evidence that He has affected history as has no other person.

In an effort to get around the division, the Pharisees asked the man's opinion of Jesus. Not knowing any more about Jesus except his own healing, the man said, "He is a prophet" (v. 17). As a desperate resort, the Pharisees, in spite of the testimony of his neighbors, questioned whether the man had ever been blind. They were seeking an escape from this dilemma. People who will not to see cannot be convinced despite the evidence.

So the Pharisees called the man's parents to determine if he was born blind. And if so, how did he now see? In turn the parents acknowledged that their son had been born blind. But they said that they did not really know how he was healed. The verb for "know" means "really to know." Though they had heard his story, they were not present when the miracle took place. So in that sense they could not speak with firsthand knowledge. So they sought to get off the hook by saying, "He is of age; ask him: he shall speak for himself"(v. 21).

Verse 22 tells the real reason for their statement. It was "because they feared the Jews: for the Jews [Sanhedrin] had agreed already, that if any man did confess that he was Christ, he should be put out of the synagogue."

To be put out of the synagogue was an awesome thing. Spiritually, it meant to be cut off from the people of God, so no salvation. Practically, such a person was ostracized socially and economically. Other Jews were not to associate with him. If he were a business man, no Jew could trade with him. If he were employed, he lost his job and could not be hired by any other Jew. Thus the parents said that if this were to happen, let it happen to their son and not to them. Some parents!

The Teacher of the Teachers (John 9:24-34)

As a last resort, the Pharisees once again called in the healed man. Due to the parents' testimony they could no longer question that a miracle had been performed. So they tried to put pressure on the man to agree with their view that Jesus was a sinner (v. 24). Thus there began a battle of wits. The Pharisees, who were experts in debate, found that they were only half-armed. A. T. Robertson was fond of saying that the Pharisees could split a hair six ways and still have some hair left. But in this case, they ran out of hair!

"Give God the praise" was one way of putting a witness under oath. Then they made the flat statement, "We know that this man is a sinner" (v. 24). The verb "know" renders a verb that means "to know by perception." In effect, they said, "We have studied the experiential knowledge about Jesus, and we have concluded with full understanding that He is a sinner."

The man had more courage than his parents. His reply is one of the greatest statements in the Bible. It deserves to stand alongside the answer Peter and John gave to the Sanhedrin. When forbidden to teach in the name of Jesus Christ, they said, "Whether it be right in the sight of God to hearken unto you more than unto God, judge ye. For we cannot but speak the things which we have seen and heard" (Acts 4:19-20).

The healed man said, "Whether he be a sinner or no, I know not: one thing I know, that, whereas I was blind, now I see" (v. 25).

"Know" in each case translates the same verb used by the Pharisees in verse 24. In effect, he said, "I too have had experiential knowledge concerning Jesus. I have weighed the evidence and have come to the firm conclusion that, regardless of what you know, I know with conviction that whereas I was blind, now I see."

Actually, the man was toying with his adversaries. He said he was no theologian. He knew nothing about their hair-splitting theology, but he had had an experience with Jesus that could not be shaken by any of their arguments. All of their theological jumbo could not close again his once-blinded eyes. The difference between the Pharisees and this man was that they had experiential knowledge *about* Jesus; the healed man had knowledge born of an experience *with* Jesus. Some skeptics may argue against our logic, but they cannot argue successfully against our experience with Jesus.

Unable to discount the man's experience, the Pharisees asked him how Jesus opened his eyes (v. 26). Since they had no answer for the healed man's experience, they stalled for time. What they did not know was that they had led with their chins, and the healed man was quick to seize the advantage. Taunting them he said he had told them, but evidently they had not heard him. "Wherefore would ye hear it again? will ye also be his disciples?" (v. 27). Literally he inquired, "Not also you of all people are willing his disciples to become?" Note the emphatic use of "ye." He knew that this was the last thing they had in mind. So he was making fun of them.

Striking back, they said, literally, "You on your part are that one's disciple; but we on our part are disciples of Moses. We know that God spoke unto Moses: as for this fellow, we know not from whence He is" (vv. 28-29). The Pharisees did not so much as call Jesus by name. They referred to Him as that one and this one ("fellow" not in the Greek text). They knew Jesus' name, so this was a deliberate slur. To them He was a nonentity. They said, literally, "We ourselves really know that to Moses God spoke; but this one we do not really know whence He is. The tense of "spoke" means "a complete, final speaking." They flatly denied Jesus' claim that God spoke through Him. As for not knowing whence Jesus came, certainly the people of Jerusalem knew or thought they did (John 7:27). Apparently the Pharisees also knew of Jesus' Galilean residence (John 7:52). So, these Pharisees merely pretended not to know this for argument's sake. We may assume that they were ignorant as to Jesus' virgin birth in Bethlehem. Indeed, they probably held to a false report that Jesus was born out of wedlock (see John 8:41).

But their claim of ignorance as to Jesus' origin was thrown back into their faces. The healed man was alert to any opening and swiftly took advantage of it. "Why herein is a marvellous thing, that ye know not from whence he is, and yet he hath opened mine eyes" (v. 30).

This fellow was having a field day. Jesus had healed his blindness, yet the religious authorities professed ignorance concerning Him! In effect, the man said, "You fellows are supposed to be informed about such matters. You need to do your homework. A man with such power, and you have not checked up on Him! Ridiculous!"

However, he was not content to stop there. "Now we know that God heareth not sinners" (v. 31). The Pharisees would have to say amen to that. But note "we." This is not an editorial *we*. At this point, the former blind beggar dared to identify himself with these teachers of Israel (see Matt. 23:2). In fact, having bested the master debaters in debate, he proceeded to teach the teachers. This was to them the ultimate in insults.

"But if any man be a worshipper of God, and doeth his will, him he heareth" (v. 31). Again, the Pharisees must say amen. They had called Jesus a sinner. But now the man's description might be one of Jesus. So the Pharisees were caught on the horns of a dilemma. Either they must deny their own theology or they must admit that Jesus was not a sinner. Either way they replied, they were discredited before the Jewish people. They had painted themselves into a corner from which there was no escape.

But the man was not through. He proceeded to pour salt into their wounds. "Since the world began was it not heard that any man opened the eyes of one that was born blind. If this man were not of God, he could do nothing" (vv. 32-33). Jesus had done this unheard of thing. Whence came His power? From Satan? Or from God? The Pharisees did not answer the question. Certainly they would not attribute such a good work to Satan. Yet if Jesus were a sinner, He must have acted under Satan's power. They could not admit that. They refused to admit that Jesus came from God. They gave no answer because they had none. No wonder that we say that this simple man of faith had confounded the scholars.

There are but three answers to an unanswerable argument: agree with the opponent, ridicule him or her, or answer with violence. The Pharisees chose the second and third (v. 34). They ridiculed him. "Thou wast altogether born in sins, and dost thou teach us?" Then they used violence: "They cast him out." Literally, "They cast him out [outside]." This does not mean casting him out of the synagogue. Only a formal meeting of the Sanhedrin could do that. They used mob violence. They cast him out of their presence.

In logic, if you start with the wrong premise, no matter how skillfully you argue, you reach the wrong conclusion. The Pharisees' false premise was that Jesus was a sinner because He performed even a good deed on the Sabbath Day. Even in reason, they were confounded by a simple man who had had an experience with Christ—truth was on his side. The result was that they had to resort to ridicule and violence rather than to agree with their opponent.

The Pharisees are still with us in those who set their wills against Jesus Christ. So take a lesson from this healed man. Have a definite spiritual experience with Christ; stand by it; and let truth be your buckler, shield, and weapon. Instead of defending the Bible, declare it. Error may win some skirmishes, but it will never win the war. Do not fear to let truth do battle with falsehood in life's arena. Truth will win every time!

7
Was Jesus God?

(John 10:22-38)

"I and my Father are one" (John 10:30).

Throughout the Christian era there has existed a struggle among theologians as to the nature of Jesus Christ. Was He God? Was He man? Or was He the God-Man or God in human form?

Perhaps the greatest of these controversies was the Arian controversy in the fourth century A.D. A man named Arius held that Christ was not of the same substance with God, but He was of like substance. The difference in the spelling of the two Greek words was what we call *i* or an *iota* subscript, an *i* written below the line. Arius was opposed by Athanasius. It was said that the Christian world was divided by an *iota* subscript. Arius's view that Christ was of like substance held that Christ was a created being and less than God. Athanasius said that Christ was of the same substance or God in flesh. In A.D. 325 the Council of Nicaea decided in favor of Christ being of the same substance with God. Arius's view continued to gain followers, especially in the eastern part of the empire. At one point it seemed that Arius and his like substance view would prevail, but at the Council of Constantinople in A.D. 381, the decision of the Council of Nicaea was ratified.

This settled the matter for the time being. But there are still some who question the full deity-humanity of Jesus Christ. The purpose of this message is to show that Jesus did indeed declare His oneness with God the Father.

Demand for Identity (John 10:22-24)

Following the Feast of Tabernacles Jesus left Jerusalem for a ministry in Judea. Almost three months separate verses 21 and 22. Luke 10:1—13:21 records this ministry.

Now Jesus was back in Jerusalem for the Feast of Dedication. It is called Hanukkah, coming around our Christmas season. Antiochus Epiphanes, the Seleucid king in Antioch, had defiled the Jewish temple by sacrificing a sow on the sacred altar. The body was boiled in a large pot. Then the residue was used to sprinkle the temple walls, thus totally defiling it. This act provoked a victorious Jewish rebellion led by Judas Maccabees. In 165 B.C. the temple was cleansed and rededicated. The Feast of Dedication commemorated this event. Since it was one of the lesser feasts, Jesus probably would not have attended it had He not been in nearby Judea. John noted that "it was winter" (v. 22), the rainy season.

This explains why Jesus was walking on Solomon's Porch, a covered, colonnaded area running the full length of the temple area on the eastern side. It was at this time that the Jewish religious leaders, literally, suddenly formed a circle about Jesus (v. 24). Doing so, they made a demand. "How long dost thou make us to doubt? If thou be the Christ, tell us plainly." Literally they said, "Until when do you lift up our souls." They were still fretting over their verbal defeat during the Feast of Tabernacles. He had held them in suspense.

Jesus had deliberately avoided using the term "Christ" in public. The Jewish idea was that of a political-military figure. He would lead a revolt, throw off the Roman yoke, and establish His kingdom in which—with Him—the Jews would rule the world. Jesus avoided use of "Son of David" for the same reason.

If only He would say, "I am the Christ," they could charge Him before Pilate as a threat to Roman supremacy. It was now only a few months before Jesus' death. His popularity with the people was great. So the rulers were desperate for grounds on which to charge Jesus.

Jesus had called Himself the Son of God. But His favorite term of self-designation was "Son of man." It had messianic connotations but without the political-military aspect. But, as always, He refused to be drawn into their trap.

Jesus came to establish a spiritual kingdom in people's hearts. This calls for a Suffering Servant Messiah, not a political-military Messiah. His kingdom is to be spread through proclaiming the gospel, "the sword of the Spirit, which is the word of God" (Eph. 6:17).

No, Jesus did not pose as a political-military Messiah. Neither should His followers assume such a role in an endeavor to achieve spiritual goals.

Jesus' Identity of Himself (John 10:25-33)

When I was elected president of the Southern Baptist Convention, I soon learned a lesson. In a news interview I never answered a question with yes or no. If I did, some newspersons would make their questions a direct quote from me. So I reworded the question in my answer.

Jesus did this in reply to the question from these Jewish leaders. To "If thou be the Christ, tell us plainly," He did not say yes or no. Instead, He replied in His own way and time. What He said left no doubt that He was the Christ. But He did not simply say yes. Indeed, He said far more.

Jesus began by reminding them that He had told them previously who He was, but they refused to believe Him. Furthermore, His works done in His Father's name had not evoked their faith (vv. 25-26a).

Then Jesus reopened the matter of His being the Good Shepherd, about which they had debated during His visit three months previously (John 10:7-18). They had not believed in Him because they were not His sheep. "My sheep hear my voice, and I know them, and they follow me" (v. 27).

Leo Eddleman tells of an experience he had while serving as a missionary in Israel. One day he was at a well to which shepherds brought their flocks. The sheep were mingled together. When one shepherd was ready to leave, he started walking, uttering a certain sound. Immediately, his sheep came out of the mingled mass and followed him. As always, Jesus had drawn a lesson from a real life scene.

Then Jesus made a tremendous statement: "I give unto them eternal life; and they shall never perish, neither shall any man pluck [snatch] them out of my hand. My Father, which gave them me, is greater than all; and no man is able to pluck them out of my Father's hand" (vv. 28-29).

Here is one of the great passages on the security of the believer. And it came from Jesus Himself! "Perish" renders a verb from whence comes the name Apollyon, one name of the devil. It may mean to go to hell. "Never" translates a double negative. In English, a double negative makes a positive. If one says, "I have not got no money," it means "I have some money." One time I made this point in a sermon. Afterward a man said to me, "Preacher, if I say I ain't got no money, I ain't got no money." Good economics, but poor grammar.

But in Greek, a double negative makes a stronger negative. The man was speaking in Greek and did not know it. Literally, Jesus said, "Most certainly, no one of My sheep will go to hell." "Neither" renders a strong negative. So again, "Most certainly, no one snatches them out of My hand." Furthermore, His Father is greater than all, and, literally, "Nothing [man, devil, or thing] is powerful [enough] to snatch them out of my Father's hand."

When my son was just a toddler, he and I would walk on the sidewalk outside our home. The sidewalk was made of octagon-shaped concrete blocks. The roots of large trees had pushed them up in spots. As we walked, he would hold on to one of my fingers, but I held him by his wrist. When his little feet stumbled over the rough places, his weak hand would lose hold of my finger. But he did not fall, for his father was holding his wrist.

So it is with us. We may stumble, lose our grip on our Heavenly Father, but we do not fall. He is holding on to us.

In Colossians 3:3 Paul said, "For ye are dead [to the old life of sin], and your life [salvation life] is hid with Christ in God." "Is hid" translates a verb that has in it the idea of a lock. So our salvation life is protected by a double lock: with Christ, in God. A. T. Robertson said that no hellish burglar can ever break those locks.

Then Jesus gave His plain answer to the Pharisees' question, "I and my Father are one" (v. 30). Jesus mentioned Himself first because the question concerned His identity. Note that He still did not use the word *Christ*. But He said more. He asserted His identity and equality with the Father. In plain words Jesus claimed to be God in flesh (see John 1:1,14).

To the Jews, this was blatant blasphemy, punishable by death by stoning (v. 31). There were no stones on Solomon's Porch, but so enraged were these Jewish leaders that they went after stones. Jesus asked for which of His good works were they planning to stone Him (v. 32).

"The Jews answered him, saying, For a good work we stone thee not; but for blasphemy; and because that thou, being a man, makest thyself God" (v. 33). In John 5:18 the charge was "making himself equal with God." But here it is "being a man, makest thyself God."

Some modern theologians may miss the point. But those theologians on the spot did not miss it. Definitely, Jesus called Himself God!

Proof of Jesus' Deity (John 10:34-38)

Jesus was in dire peril. The Jewish rulers had murder in their eyes. Since His first visit to Jerusalem in His public ministry, the Jewish leaders had opposed Him. In each subsequent visit, their opposition became more venomous. This was the worst. His "hour" had not yet come. Jesus would die, but it would be according to the Father's will, not from mob violence. So immediately following this incident He left Jerusalem, not to return until His time had come (vv. 39-42). However, before departing, He justified His claim to deity.

Jesus first appealed to the Scriptures. Assuming that these Jews were Pharisees, this was the ultimate in authority. He quoted from Psalm 82:6 where unjust judges were called "gods." If this be true, He asked, why then did they propose to stone Him for blasphemy because He claimed to be God? (vv. 35-36). Because, as they would agree, "the scripture cannot be broken." These judges were unjust. But Jesus is the One "whom the Father hath sanctified [set apart for God's service], and sent into the world." Of course, these Jews would deny this claim.

So Jesus cited His works as evidence that this was true (vv. 37-38). "If I do not the works of my Father, believe me not. But if I do, though ye believe not me, believe the works: that ye may know, and believe, that the Father is in me, and I in him."

"If I do" (v. 38) expresses a condition assumed as being true. And even though people do not believe in Him as a person, by the works He does, literally, they may come to know, and keep on believing that He and the Father are one. Only minds prejudiced hopelessly against Jesus can deny that Jesus did the works of God.

So we return to our question: Was Jesus God? He certainly and emphatically declared that He was. Either He was an extreme fanatic and guilty of the worst of blasphemies or else He was who He said He was/is. History gives a resounding yes to the latter.

There is yet one more question to answer, and no one but you can answer it. *Who is Jesus to you?* The Bible presents Him as God's virgin-born Son, God Himself in flesh for human redemption. History declares Him to be the greatest Person who ever lived. He is the supreme Teacher and perfect Example in doing God's will. All of these are important beyond the ability of human language to express.

What is your personal relationship to Him? In the final analysis, for you that is the supreme question. How you answer it determines the quality of life you live on this earth and in the ever-unfolding eternity beyond. I pray that you will receive Him as your Lord and Savior. For anything less than this is to deny Him. Your acceptance or denial of Him has eternal consequences!

8

Throwing Down the Gauntlet

(John 11:1-54)

"Then from that day forth they took counsel together for to put him to death" (John 11:53).

From the time that Jesus left Nazareth to embark upon His public ministry, He never had a home of His own. Thus Jesus could say, "Foxes have holes, and birds of the air have nests; but the Son of man hath not where to lay his head" (Luke 9:58). But if He had a home away from home, none could qualify more than that of Martha, Mary, and Lazarus, located in Bethany, just over the crest of the Mount of Olives. As a bird flies, it was little more than a stone's throw from the temple area in Jerusalem, the center of power for the Jewish religious leaders. This home in Bethany is the center of events in John 11.

Of course, John's overall purpose in writing his Gospel was to show that Jesus Christ is the Son of God in whom we may have eternal life through faith in Him (John 20:31). To prove his point, John built his Gospel around seven "signs" or miracles performed by Jesus. The seventh and greatest of these signs took place in Bethany.

But throughout this Gospel, we find that John had secondary purposes in the selection of his material. For instance, Jesus' changing water into wine was to teach the superiority of God's revelation in Christ over that of the old covenant. The healing of the lame man at the pool of Bethesda marks the beginning of the Sabbath controversy. The feeding of the five thousand gives the backdrop for the collapse of Jesus' Galilean ministry.

John 11 seems to have a secondary and a tertiary purpose. The apostle showed a different side to Martha than the one in Luke 10:38-42. And most of all, Jesus threw down the gauntlet to the Sadducees who denied the resurrection from the dead.

The Crisis in Bethany (John 11:1-17)

If there was one home in all Palestine that should have been free of trouble and sorrow, one would have expected it to be the home of Jesus' special friends in Bethany. It was Jesus' home away from home. To Him the latch string was always on the outside. As we once said, "It was the 'Preacher's home.'"

But God does not seal His own in trouble-proof plastic bags. As the old Spanish proverb said, "Sooner or later every house will have its hush." Or in Longfellow's words in "The Rainy Day," "Into each life some rain will fall, / Some days will be dark and dreary."

Such happened to the home in Bethany (vv. 1-2). Lazarus was ill, so ill in fact, that Martha and Mary sent for Jesus. "Lord, behold, he whom thou lovest is sick" (v. 3). "Lovest" expresses the warm love of friendship.

Now at this time Jesus was in Perea, a two-day journey from Bethany. When the messenger arrived with the news, Jesus said that Lazarus's illness was not unto death but for the glory of God and "that the Son of God might be glorified thereby" (v. 4). As a matter of fact, Lazarus did die. But Jesus knew He would raise him from the dead. Thus, God would be glorified. But in Jesus' case, "be glorified" in John refers to the crucifixion. Thus we see John's purpose in recording this chapter. What He did in Bethany would be directly related to His crucifixion.

Resuming the narrative, John said that Jesus "loved" this family. "Loved" translates the word for divine love. We would expect Jesus to start toward Bethany immediately. Instead, He remained where He was for two days (vv. 5-6). Then He proposed that He and the apostles leave for Judea. But they reminded Him that one reason for their being in Perea was because the Jewish leaders wanted to kill Him (vv. 7-8).

But Jesus said that Lazarus was sleeping, and He must go and awaken him. The apostles said that his sleeping was evidence that he was improving. Then Jesus said, "Lazarus is dead" (v. 14).

Some see this idea of sleeping as evidence that in death the soul remains in an unconscious state until the resurrection. However, the Jews, Romans, and Greeks used this term as a euphemism for death, even as we do today. In fact, the Greek word *sleepeth* comes over into English as "cemetery." At this time Lazarus was dead and buried.

When Jesus insisted on going to Bethany, Thomas said to the other apostles, "Let us also go, that we may die with him" (v. 16). Here we see a side of Thomas that is almost altogether overlooked. Did you ever hear him referred to as Heroic Thomas? Or Loyal Thomas? Or for that matter as Inquisitive Thomas? (John 14:5). No, he is known only as Doubting Thomas (John 20:25). This suggests that we should never judge a person by one deed or by one facet of one's nature, but by the whole of one's life.

So Jesus and the apostles went to Bethany. Arriving there they found that Lazarus "had lain in the grave four days already" (v. 17).

Now let us do a little arithmetic. It took two days for the messenger to go from Bethany to Perea. Jesus tarried two days in Perea after receiving the news of Lazarus's illness. Two additional days were required for Him to reach Bethany. The four days following the arrival of the messenger correspond to the four days Lazarus had lain in his tomb. Jews buried people on the day they died, so Jesus knew that His friend was already dead when He received the news from Bethany. This in part explains why Jesus did not rush to Bethany the moment He received the news from Martha and Mary. Presently we will see that it involved even more.

Our Lord never acted without a purpose. Neither did He do so then. We often get impatient when God does not act according to our timetables. But the Eternal does not act according to our concept of time but according to His purpose. However, we often fret, only to learn that God has a greater blessing in store for us.

The Tale of Two Sisters (John 11:18-37)

From Luke's account of Jesus' visit in the home in Bethany has come the concept that Mary was the more spiritual of the two sisters, while Martha was the more practical one. In fact, Martha is seen as only a good cook. How often have I heard some lady say, "Now, Pastor, I am not a Mary; I'm a Martha." Meaning, of course, that I was not to ask her to teach, fill any leadership role in the church, or pray in public. But if we wanted someone to cook a meal, she was the one.

Now one can see these differences in Luke's Gospel. Probably by the time John wrote his Gospel these sisters were dead. Thus one purpose of John was to reveal another side of Martha. Frankly, of the two sisters, Martha is my favorite. I suppose it is because I married a Martha. One night I preached for Jess Moody when he was pastor at First Baptist Church, West Palm Beach, Florida. Jess has a gift for words. He introduced Frances by saying, "She is as delicate as an orchid and as practical as an eggbeater." I lived with her for fifty-seven-and-a-half years and could not have described her better.

Frances was an excellent cook. She enjoyed cooking. She was also a practical businesswoman. In fact, at my request she handled the business details of our family, and she did it well. Oh, she would confer with me on the more important matters, but usually I agreed with her judgment.

She used to tease me. For several years I was chairman of the Program Committee of the Southern Baptist Executive Committee. One responsibility of this committee was to recommend allocation of funds for the various agencies of the Convention. Frances would say, "You go to Nashville and deal in millions of dollars. But you want nothing to do with our nickel-and-dime budget at home."

But Frances also was a deeply spiritual person: a good teacher, leader, and counselor; she had a deep prayer life and a strong faith in the Lord. We see such characteristics in Martha.

While "Mary sat still in the house" (v. 20), grieving, Martha was stirring about seeing to the needs of guests who had come to mourn with them. Hearing that Jesus was coming up the road, she ran to greet Him. She said, "Lord, if thou hadst been here, my brother had not died. But I know, that even now, whatsoever thou wilt ask of God, God will give it thee" (vv. 21-22). Despite what had happened, she still had faith in Jesus. Indeed, one may see a slight hint that He could restore Lazarus to life.

To Jesus' assurance that her brother would rise again, Martha replied, "I know that he shall rise again in the resurrection at the last day" (v. 24). With a little imagination one may detect a note of impatience in her voice. "Oh, I know that! But what about now?"

Then Jesus uttered words that have been a pillow on which countless millions have rested their faith. "I am the resurrection, and the life: he that believeth in me, though he were dead, yet shall he live: And whosoever liveth and believeth in me shall never die. Believest thou this?" (vv. 25-26). Martha thought she was dwelling in the atmosphere of death when all the time she was in the presence of Life.

At this point, Martha made the greatest confession of Jesus' messiahship on record. Literally Martha said, "Yes, Lord, I have believed and continue to believe completely that You are the Christ, the Son of God, the one coming into the world" (v. 27).

When Peter made his great confession, he was on a mountaintop spiritually. But Martha was in the pit of despondency. Yet out of that pit she uttered a firmly fixed faith in her Lord. Under the circumstances, it required more faith than Peter's confession.

Yes, Martha was practical, but she also was deeply spiritual. In other words, it is not either/or but both/and.

With this, Martha told Mary that Jesus had arrived. Mary rushed to Him and fell at His feet. Like her sister, she said, "Lord, if thou hadst been here, my brother had not died" (v. 32). These sisters probably had said this many times to each other. But, unlike Martha, Mary did not express faith as to the future. She loved Jesus and believed in Him, but apparently she lacked the rugged character of her sister.

Jesus asked to be taken to the tomb. John 11:35 is the shortest verse in the Bible: "Jesus wept." Literally, He "burst into tears." Why did He do this? Some see it as personal grief over Lazarus's death. However, Jesus knew He was going to raise him. Others see

Him weeping for Lazarus, knowing that He was about to call him back from the bliss of heaven to endure further the rigors of an earthly life. I see it as His sympathetic reaction to the grief of others. "His heart is touched with your grief."[1]

But there was a mixed reaction in the crowd. Some noted how much Jesus loved Lazarus. Others cynically asked why He who had healed the blind could not have prevented Lazarus's death. Two groups of people saw the same thing, but with different reactions. The difference was not in Jesus but in them.

The Miracle at Bethany (John 11:38-46)

Lazarus was buried in a cave with a stone rolled across the entrance. So, arriving at the tomb, Jesus told those present to remove the stone (v. 39a). Note that He let people do what they could do, and He left to Himself what only He could do. Someone said that God never does through a miracle what He can do through an individual.

It was at this point that Martha's practical nature came to the forefront. She said, "Lord, by this time he stinketh: for he hath been dead four days" (v. 39).

Thus we come back to the four days and the reason for Jesus' delay in coming to Bethany. He knew all along what He was going to do, but there must be no question about its nature. Among the Jews were those who held to the belief that when a person dies, the spirit lingers about the body for three days in hopes of reentering it. If at the end of this time, that had not happened, the spirit left. Had Jesus raised Lazarus on the third day, these people would have said, "This is nothing special. This is simply what we have said all along!"

So there must be no doubt. It was on the fourth day. The body was already beginning to decay. Lazarus was dead! It was nothing less than a miracle—a work of God!

After thanking the Father for granting His prayer even before He prayed it, Jesus "cried with a loud voice, Lazarus, come forth" (v. 43). The loud voice was not for Lazarus's benefit. It was so the crowd could hear Jesus and know that the dead arose at His word.

And he came forth, bound in his grave clothes. Jesus said, "Loose him, and let him go" (v. 44).

It should be noted, however, that the raising of Lazarus was not a resurrection. Jesus is the "firstfruits" of which our resurrection at the end of the age will be the general harvest (1 Cor. 15:23). Resurrection means to rise from the dead to die no more. Lazarus, Jairus's daughter, and the widow's son at Nain were brought back from the dead, but later they died again. So what happened to them was a resuscitation. The dictionary defines this word two ways: (1) to revive bodily functions such as breathing into lungs until they work on their own or massaging a heart until it beats on its own; (2) to bring back from the dead. Lazarus's resuscitation occurred in the second sense.

Again there were differing reactions to Jesus's miracle (vv. 45-46). Some who saw it believed in Jesus. Others ran to tell the Pharisees. Since the Pharisees believed in the resurrection, contrary to the Sadducees, we would expect them to welcome the news. But so adamant was their opposition to Jesus that they forgot their theological differences in order to accomplish their common demonic end. Truly, politics makes strange bedfellows.

The Fatal Decision (John 11:47-53)

Jesus had raised the dead in Galilee. When news of this reached Jerusalem, the Jewish leaders could easily deny it. They looked upon Galileans as "country bumpkins" who would believe anything. When Jesus raised Lazarus within two miles of the temple and many people of Jerusalem witnessed it, there could be no more denials. The one inevitable fact was that Jesus must be destroyed.

"Then gathered the chief priests and the Pharisees a council" (v. 47). This was a formal meeting of the Sanhedrin. Jesus was doing many miracles, even raising the dead right under their noses. "What do we?" was really directed to the Pharisees. Up until this time the Sadducees had let the Pharisees carry the responsibility of stopping Jesus. The role of the Sadducees in this regard was minor, lending a hand on occasion. And the Pharisees had failed.

The Pharisees were great on debate but short on action. If left to themselves, it is doubtful that they would have killed Jesus. They might have argued Him to death, but no more. Even when they thought to stone Him, they had failed. But when the realistic Sadducees took charge, it was quite another matter. They were more interested in politics than in religion. They worked hand in glove with the Romans, enjoying power and prosperity thereby. The words in verse 48 most likely came from them.

If Jesus was not stopped, a revolution was inevitable, so they thought. "And the Romans shall come and take away both our place and nation." Note "place" (their privileged position) before "nation." Demagogues always clothe their selfish desires in some noble language.

Then the high priest Caiaphas, a Sadducee, took charge (vv. 49-50). He said it would be better for one man to die rather than for the nation to perish. That is, so long as that man was not Caiaphas. So under the false colors of patriotism the Sanhedrin agreed that Jesus must die. In raising Lazarus Jesus had thrown down the gauntlet. And the Sanhedrin picked it up. In a sense Jesus said, "Put up or shut up."

"Then from that day forth they took counsel together [Pharisees and Sadducees] for to put him to death" (v. 53). This was about three months before Jesus' death.

John added his comment that unknowingly Caiaphas prophesied the manner of Jesus' death. However, it was not for the Jewish nation alone, but for the whole world (vv. 51-52).

Yes, Jesus died to provide redemption for all people. But, according to the old saying, "The same sun that softens wax, hardens mud."

We call Jesus's raising of Lazarus His greatest miracle. But we should say His greatest, except one. His greatest miracle is that He takes those who are dead in sin and makes them alive in Him forevermore. The final result depends upon you.

Are you wax or mud? Your reaction to Jesus gives the answer.

---

1. B. B. McKinney, "Have Faith in God," *Baptist Hymnal* (Nashville: Convention Press, 1975), No. 376. © Copyright 1934 Renewal 1962 Broadman Press. All rights reserved.

9

Two Questions, Two Destinies

(John 12:1-19)

"Then took Mary a pound of ointment of spikenard, very costly, and anointed the feet of Jesus, and wiped his feet with her hair: and the house was filled with the odour of the ointment.

"Then saith one of his disciples, Judas Iscariot, Simon's son, which should betray him,

"Why was not this ointment sold for three hundred pence, and given to the poor?" (John 12:3-5)

Each one of you can look into your past and see some moment or some event that marked the direction your life would take for better or for worse. In most cases, it was the culmination of all that came prior to that time.

With Abraham, it was his response to God's call to leave country and family to go into a foreign land from which he never returned (Gen. 12:1). With Moses, it was his burning bush experience (Ex. 3). In Isaiah's case, it was his temple vision following Uzziah's death (Isa. 6). In Paul's case, it was his Damascus road encounter with the risen Christ (Acts 9).

The purpose of this sermon is to study two other biblical characters and the decisions they made concerning Jesus: one to her eternal glory; the other to his eternal shame. You may well ask yourself, "With which of these two do I stand?"

The Feast in Bethany (John 12:1-2)

It was the feast of the Passover in A.D. 30. Jesus arrived in Bethany six days before the Passover or on Friday afternoon (v. 1).

John said that "they made him a supper" (v. 2). True to her nature, Martha helped with the meal. Lazarus also was a guest. The
meal probably honored him along with Jesus because Jesus had
raised him from the dead. Matthew and Mark recorded this supper,
stating that it was in the home of Simon, the leper. Since the other
writers mentioned this, John did not name the host. But he supple-
mented their accounts by including the names of those omitted by
the Synoptic Gospels. The omission of the names of Lazarus, Martha, and Mary may be explained by assuming that they were still
living when Matthew and Mark wrote their Gospels. To have mentioned them by name could have endangered their lives. But by the
time that John wrote, they probably had died. Thus they could be
named with impunity.

If we had only John's account, it would appear that this event took
place on Friday evening. This is hardly likely because it would be the
Jewish Sabbath, which began at sunset on Friday. Matthew and
Mark placed this supper on Tuesday night after Jesus had spent the
day in controversy with the Jewish leaders. This is probably the correct time of the meal. Apparently John recorded it at this point since
it is his final mention of Bethany.

Assuming that the Synoptic Gospels are correct as to the time, on
the previous Sunday Jesus had made His royal entry into Jerusalem
(John 12:12-19). The crowds hailed Him with messianic cries. Jesus
presented Himself as the King, but He was subsequently rejected by
the Jews.

This rejection is significant. For Jews from all over the known
world were present. No matter where Jews lived, they hoped at least
one time to observe this feast in Jerusalem.

Twenty years after Jesus' death a Roman governor had a census
made as to the number of lambs sacrificed at that Passover. The
number was two hundred and fifty thousand. Since one lamb was
slain for every ten people, this means that two and one-half million
Jews attended that feast.

Assuming this to be typical, a like number could have been
present at this time. So in a sense, Jesus was not rejected by a small
number of Palestinian Jews. He was rejected by world Jewry.

The Events at the Supper (John 12:3-8)

According to the custom of the time, the guests reclined on couches about the table. Let us assume that Simon the leper sat in the place for the host. If so, then as the guest of primary honor, Jesus reclined on his right. As the guest of secondary honor, Lazarus would have reclined on Simon's left.

All three of these Gospels relate that during the meal a woman entered and anointed Jesus with an ointment of spikenard. John added that she also wiped His feet with her hair (v. 3). These Gospels also record the complaint made about this "waste." Many people consider money spent for spiritual purposes as a waste. Matthew, Mark, and John also record a rebuke from Jesus about the complaint. But let us examine in detail the account given by John.

John mentioned that this anointing was done by Mary. This was typical of her. This ointment of spikenard was the oil of nard, a fragrant oil that comes from an East Indian plant. It is described as very precious or costly. Nard was considered a gift fit for a king. Herodotus listed it among gifts sent by Cambyses to the king of Ethiopia. Evidently, it was Mary's most precious possession. So her act was one of great love and sacrifice.

In reply to Judas's rebuke of Mary, Jesus said, "Let her alone: against the day of my burying hath she kept this" (v. 7). In Matthew 26:13 it is recorded that Jesus said, "Wheresoever this gospel shall be preached in the whole world, there shall also this, that this woman hath done, be told for a memorial of her." Without John's Gospel this would be a nameless memorial.

The odor of the ointment filled the house (v. 3). But it did more. On the wings of the gospel it has been wafted throughout the world as a memorial to a woman who rendered a loving service to Jesus. And in every such deed of unselfish service rendered in His name, one can still catch a scent of this oil of spikenard.

John also named Judas as the one who criticized Mary. Of interest is the fact that he is always mentioned as the one who betrayed Jesus. Said he, "Why was not this ointment sold for three hundred pence, and given to the poor?" (v. 5). "Pence" translates *dēnarius*, a coin worth about seventeen cents, but it had greater purchasing power than now. So the amount was about fifty-one dollars.

John added that Judas did not care for the poor. He was a thief who carried the money bag for Jesus and the apostles and stole from it. He wanted the fifty-one dollars for himself (v. 6). Judas was materialism personified. His only concern was for himself.

Immediately following this supper Judas went to the chief priests (Sadducees) and bargained to betray Jesus (Matt. 26:14-15; Mark 14:10-11). Note that he did not set a price for his treachery. "What will ye give me, and I will deliver him unto you?" (Matt. 26:15). In dealing with the devil, he sets the price. And when Judas failed to get his hands on the fifty-one dollars, he accepted thirty pieces of silver worth about twenty-five dollars. But it is from John that we learn the immediate reason for Judas's act. Jesus' rebuke triggered his resentment into the unlawful deed.

What may we say about Judas? Jesus chose him as an apostle, but why? Some say that he was chosen for the very purpose of betrayal, that he was even born for that purpose. However, such an idea is contrary to the very nature of God. Jesus said that Judas was responsible for his act (Matt. 26:24). Rather than being a puppet on the string of fate, Judas was a person endowed with the right of choice. At the same time, he was responsible for his choices. In trying to clear Judas, we malign God.

Perhaps Jesus saw in him, as in the other apostles, qualities that, if surrendered to Him, would be valuable in the infant Christian movement. But Judas never surrendered himself to Jesus. One year before Judas betrayed Jesus, our Lord said, "One of you is a devil" (John 6:70). John notes that He spoke of Judas (v. 71). Note that he "is a devil," not was a devil when Jesus chose him. It is entirely possible that Judas fomented the attempt to make Jesus a king, a political-military messiah following the feeding of the multitude. In any case, Jesus saw that the devil was working on Judas.

One thing is certain. Judas was never a Christian. This is evident in the upper room when Jesus said that one of the twelve would betray Him. One by one the apostles asked, "Lord, is it I?" (Matt. 26:22). This form of question invited a negative answer. We would ask, "It isn't I, is it, Lord?" Finally, Judas asked the same question except that he addressed Jesus as "Master" or rabbi (Matt. 26:25). Even in his act of betrayal he called Jesus master (Matt. 26:49). There is no evidence that he ever called Jesus Lord. In his question Judas knew that he was the traitor, only he hoped that Jesus did not know it.

In addition to the above example, many other efforts have been made to clear Judas of blame. Some hold that he was an agent of the Sanhedrin who infiltrated the twelve for the purpose of betraying Jesus. But there is no evidence to support this view. Others would make him a super-Christian who sought to force Jesus into a situation where He would have to declare His messiahship and set up His kingdom. Still others would make Judas a superpatriot who betrayed Jesus in order to prevent a revolution that would bring Rome's wrath down on his nation. All these efforts are based on sentiment, not on Scripture.

Judas will ever remain a mystery. There is an old statement that people name their boys after Paul and their dogs after Nero. But the only thing of which I am aware that is named after Judas is the "Judas goat" used in some packing houses to lead sheep to the slaughter. Judas carried an honored name. The Jewish hero of the period between the Old and New Testaments was Judas Maccabaeus. One of Jesus' half-brothers was named Judas or Jude. Judas Iscariot dragged this name into the dust.

In spite of all efforts to absolve him from guilt, he will always be known as "Judas Iscariot, Simon's son, which should betray him" (John 12:4).

The Reactions in the Crisis

As we read John's account of the supper, other than Jesus, two people stand out—Mary and Judas. In the overall story as recorded by Matthew, Mark, and John we see two reactions. In my judgment, Judas and Mary were the first two people fully to realize that Jesus was going to die. According to Matthew 26:2, prior to the supper Jesus predicted the very day of His death. To His apostles Jesus said, "Ye know that after two days is the feast of the passover, and the Son of man is betrayed to be crucified." According to Jewish time, Jesus was both betrayed and crucified between sunset on Thursday and sunset on Friday.

Judas heard Jesus say it. And we may be certain that Mary and others in Bethany soon knew about it. Knowing this both Mary and Judas asked a question.

Upon hearing this we may well imagine that Mary reasoned thus: "Jesus is going to die. As a woman in a man's world there is nothing I can do to prevent it." So she asked herself the question, *What can I do for Jesus?* At least she could show Him that she loved Him and understood. So she anointed Him for His burial.

At the same time Judas also realized that Jesus was going to die on a cross. There was no place in his theology for a dying Messiah. Thinking that Jesus would be a political-military messiah, he had followed Him. Judas visualized an earthly kingdom with him occupying a principal place in it. Most likely he was the prime cause for the attempt to make Jesus declare His kingdom following the feeding of the five thousand.

Passover commemorated Jehovah's deliverance of Israel from Egyptian bondage. In Jesus' day the Jews expected another deliverance from Rome at some Passover. The conflict between Jesus and the Jewish leaders was hastening to a climax. At this particular Passover, there was an air of expectancy. Surely, the messianic deliverance was at hand. On Palm Sunday Jesus had ridden into Jerusalem amid messianic cries. *Surely,* thought Judas, *this is the time.* The occasion was ripe for Jesus to declare His kingdom. Instead, He merely entered the temple, looked about, and then returned to Bethany. In Judas's mind, Jesus failed.

So, in effect, Judas said: "He is not the Messiah! He is only a rabbi who does wonderful works and says beautiful things. And now He is going to be killed. I left everything to follow Him. Now I must get what I can out of the debacle." So Judas also asked himself a question, *What can Jesus do for me?* And he betrayed Him for thirty pieces of silver.

Mary of Bethany is not mentioned again in the Bible. But Jesus' memorial to her continues through the ages. Judas? Matthew 27:3-5 says: "Then Judas which had betrayed him, when he saw that he [Jesus] was condemned, repented himself, and brought again the thirty pieces of silver to the chief priests and elders, Saying, I have sinned in that I have betrayed the innocent blood. And they said, What is that to us? see thou to that. And he cast down the pieces of silver in the temple, and departed, and went and hanged himself."

"Repented" does not translate the word for true repentance. The usual word for "repent" means "a change of mind." To the Greeks *mind* represented the whole person. Thus the meaning would be a complete change of heart, life, attitude, or of the entire direction or manner of life. Judas did not experience this. The word used here means "to be sorry" or "to regret because of the act and its consequences." In a sense he was sorry that he got caught.

The once-coveted silver turned to fire in Judas's pocket. So he sought to return it to the Sanhedrin, saying that he had betrayed innocent blood—as if he could undo what he had done. But the Sanhedrin said that it was no concern to them. That was his concern. Once they had used Judas, they cast him aside as useless. Evil always abandons its tools to their fate.

So Judas's once-grasping hands threw the blood money at their feet, went out, and hanged himself. Tradition says that he did this in the Vale of Hinnom, the garbage dump of Jerusalem that Jesus once used as a symbol of hell.

What of the thirty pieces of silver? The Sanhedrin had taken them from the temple treasury. But hypocrites that they were, they said the money could not be returned to the sacred treasury because it was tainted with blood. So they used it to purchase a potter's field in which to bury foreigners or non-Jews. Matthew said that it was called "The field of blood" (27:6-8; see also Acts 1:18-19). It might well have been called Judas's memorial cemetery.

In Acts 1:25 Peter said that Judas went to his own place. When Michelangelo painted *The Last Judgment* in the Sistine Chapel of the Vatican, he painted Judas in the lowest place in hell. With his grasping hands Judas went for it all, and he wound up with nothing except "his own place." Such is the fate of all who reject Jesus to bow before the altar of mammon.

There is also in this a lesson for Christians. Each of us lines up behind either Mary or Judas. You are either asking, "What can I do for Jesus?" or, "What can Jesus do for me?" As a Christian you have accepted what Jesus did for your salvation. Also you accept His providential care from day to day. John 1:16 reads, "Of his fulness have all we received, and grace for grace." "Fulness" denotes the very essence of His being. As such we have become children of God. All that we need for living a rich, full life we find in Christ.

"Grace for grace" means "grace face-to-face with grace" or "grace following after grace." When you were saved, God did not give you a certain amount of grace, saying to use it sparingly since that is all the grace you will ever receive. No, like manna in the wilderness, God furnishes His grace daily, each moment, the supply sufficient to your needs. And the supply is always there. As to Paul, so to you, God says, "My grace is sufficient for thee" (2 Cor. 12:9).

Yes, you are willing to receive all that the Lord does for you. But have you asked what you can do for Him? How long has it been since you sought to win a soul to faith in Him? You receive His material blessings. But do you share them with others? Where you cannot go to bear the gospel, are you giving of your means to enable others to go?

How is it in your local church? You ask what your church can do for you. Do you ask what you can do for and through your church? You want a Sunday School teacher. Are you willing to teach? You want your children to have teachers. Are you willing to teach children? You want visits from church people when you are sick? Do you visit the sick and needy? You want a pastor and other spiritual ministries and leaders. Are you giving to provide such?

Our churches need fewer sponges soaking up blessings and more springs from which blessings flow into the lives of others.

Jesus said, "I am come that they might have life, and that they might have it more abundantly" (John 10:10). "More abundantly" translates a word that means "overflowing." He came to give us salvation life, yes! But He also proposes that we have this life that overflows into the lives of others. We are not to hoard this life but to share it. We bless others out of the overflow.

The figure in this word is that of a bucket. In the bottom of the bucket is a water pipe, the other end of which is in an ever-flowing spring. As water from the spring flows into the bucket, the water level rises. Once the level reaches the top, there is no place for the water to go except to overflow.

Let us suppose that you place a bucket filled with water in a desert. Were it not for evaporation, that bucket full of water could remain in that desert a thousand years, and it would still be in a desert. But if the water keeps on overflowing, it will transform the desert into a fruitful garden.

Our world remains a spiritual desert because so many of us are content to enjoy our filled buckets of water without overflowing into the lives of others. For, I repeat, we only bless others through the overflow.

The Judas-spirit is that which receives but never shares. The Mary-spirit overflows, not counting the cost. And you and I line up either behind Judas or behind Mary. In which line do you stand?

10
Great People Can Be Humble

(John 13:1-15)

"If I then, your Lord and Master, have washed your feet; ye also ought to wash one another's feet" (John 13:14).

I attended a churchwide dinner in the First Baptist Church, Oklahoma City. During the meal I said to our guest speaker, "The wealthiest woman in Oklahoma is in this dining room. Can you pick her out?" After looking over the crowd he said he could not. Then I said, "Do you see the lady going from table to table pouring coffee? That is she." Instead of demanding a seat at the head table, she was happy to render a needed service.

She never pushed herself forward nor demanded recognition; indeed, she shunned it. But she was always there when her church needed help, financial or otherwise. She was a large stockholder in an oil company. Every time the company declared a dividend, she would call to tell me the amount of money she had to give through her church. Always she would say, "I would like for so much to go to missions. Now where do we need the rest?"

One day while she was ill, Frances and I went by to see her. When her sister took me into another room to show me something, she asked Frances, "Honey, I am rewriting my will. Do you have any suggestions?" Frances said, "Yes, I do. Herschel and I went through college during the depression of the 1930s. When our money ran out, the college had a fund established by someone from which we could get a few dollars. Without it, I doubt if we could have made it. So I have always hoped someone would establish a scholarship fund at Oklahoma Baptist University for students studying for the ministry." The lady said, "I like that." But nothing more was said. Frankly, Frances had in mind a few hundred thousand dollars.

After this dear woman's death, we learned that, after a few family bequests, she had left the remainder of her estate to establish such a fund. The immediate amount was five million dollars; eventually, it could become approximately seven million dollars! Yet she was still happy to pour coffee at a church dinner! She epitomizes the truth that *great people can afford to be humble!*

United States Senator Robert S. Kerr was a deacon in our church. Until he went to Washington he taught a class in our Sunday School. While governor of Oklahoma, if his duties carried him to other parts of the country during the week, he always flew home to teach his class on the Lord's Day. He was chairman of the board of a large oil company, and he was involved in civic affairs, government, his church, and denomination. He served one term as vice-president of the Southern Baptist Convention.

In 1951, I was president of the Southern Baptist Pastors' Conference. One day I called him from the floor of the Senate to ask if he would speak at our meeting in San Francisco. I told him he would have to pay his own expenses since we had no budget. His reply: "I consider a request from Andrew Potter [then State Executive Secretary of the Baptist General Convention of Oklahoma] and my pastor a command performance. I will be there."

After his election to the United States Senate, a national magazine carried a story about him. In it the writer told that the senator liked sorghum syrup. Shortly thereafter Kerr received a letter from a woman in New York City. She told of her liking sorghum syrup, but she had had none since leaving the South.

Not long after that, the senator made a trip to New York. While there he walked up several flights of stairs in a tenement house. In response to his knock, this lady opened the door. There before her eyes stood the United States senator holding a gallon bucket of sorghum syrup. From that event he gained the title "Sorghum Totin' Senator."

Not long before the senator's death, someone asked me whom I considered to be the two most powerful men in Washington. I said, "President John F. Kennedy and Senator Robert S. Kerr." Then he asked as to the one most powerful man in Washington. I replied, "Senator Robert S. Kerr." Asked why, I added, "The only time in the Senate that he crossed the president, he won."

Kerr's funeral was held in our church. President Kennedy was there. Vice-President and Mrs. Lyndon B. Johnson were there. Governor and Mrs. John Connally were there. In fact, just about everybody of importance in both the federal and state governments were there. I have a photograph taken from the top floor of a building across the street from our church. It shows black limousines four abreast and three blocks long used to bring the VIPs to the funeral. President Kennedy and Vice-President and Mrs. Johnson even joined the procession to the cemetery. All this for one who started out plowing a mule in southeast Oklahoma and rose to become one of the most powerful men in the nation. Yet in his spirit, he remained as humble to the end as he had been at the beginning. Yes, *great people can afford to be humble!*

I have described extensively these two people whom I was privileged to pastor. My purpose is not to glorify them. It is to say that they were both humble and devoted followers of our Lord Jesus Christ who was infinite in humility as He was in greatness. As they were finitely humble, He was infinitely humble. His entire incarnation is the supreme act of humility (Phil. 2:6-8). Our passage under consideration shows one clear example of His humility within His cosmic humiliation.

The Would-Be-Greats

In order to appreciate fully Jesus' act of humility, we must look first at these verses in Luke's Gospel. Each writer arranged his material differently. Thus Luke placed these verses following Jesus' institution of the Lord's Supper and Jesus' mention of His betrayal (Luke 22:17-23). But in *A Harmony of the Gospels*, A. T. Robertson placed them at the time Jesus and the apostles first arrived in the upper room for the Passover meal. This seems to be the proper order.

"There was also a strife among them, which of them should be accounted the greatest" (v. 24).

According to custom, they reclined on couches about the table. Since Jesus was the host, places of first and second honor at the table were respectively to the right and left of the host. So it seems that the apostles were squabbling among themselves as to who would have the place of first honor at the table. This was typical of their continuing argument as to which of them should be accounted greatest in Christ's kingdom (see Matt. 18:1-5; 20:20-28; Mark 9:33-37; 10:35-45; Luke 9:46-48).

The apostles were a motley group: fishermen, a tax collector, a zealot, and Judas, to mention only a few. Their concept of the Messiah was one who would set up an earthly kingdom. And they vied for positions of prominence in it. Despite all that Jesus had taught them, so deeply ingrained in them was this concept that, even at the solemn occasion on the very eve of Jesus's death, their wrangling for position continued.

So it is not out of order to see them at this point as ordinary men, would-be-greats seeking to obtain positions of power and prominence. This struggle was to Jesus a constant source of problems and sorrow.

Elsewhere in the New Testament, there is evidence of this struggle for position and power. Some of the Corinthian Christians even vied as to who had the most important gift of the Holy Spirit (1 Cor. 12—14). In 3 John 9-10, the apostle wrote of "Diotrephes, who loveth to have the preeminence." It is not clear whether he was a pastor or a layman. But in either case he aspired to be a church boss, something no New Testament church needs or should have. But sadly, we still have those would-be-greats in both our churches and in the broader aspects of Christianity. They are thorns in the side of both the Lord and their fellow Christians. They are sand in the gears of the Lord's work, creating strife and hindering its progress.

Jesus interrupted the apostles' argument to remind them that their attitude was pagan, not Christian. The rulers of the Gentiles or pagans lorded it over them. They were called "benefactors," but at the taxpayers' expense (v. 25).

By way of contrast, Jesus said that Christian greatness is measured by service rendered to others with no expectation of reward (vv. 26-27). So many people ask, "What is there in it for me?" That is pagan! Christians should ask, "What can I do for others as I serve the Lord?"

It has been my experience that those who contribute the most complain the least. I have always been an admirer of fine mules. So there is no disregard for human value when I cite an old saying: a pulling mule does not kick, and a kicking mule does not pull. I will let you classify yourself.

The Humility of Jesus (John 13:1-11)

In spite of their faults Jesus loved the apostles (vv. 1-3). He had been looking forward to the Passover meal, knowing that it was the last one He would eat with them (Luke 22:15). John took up the account at the close of this meal (v. 2).

In that day, people wore open sandals. And even though one invited to a meal took a bath before starting to the home of the host, he or she arrived with dusty feet. So it was customary for a slave of the host to rinse the dust from the feet of arriving guests. This was such a demeaning task that it was assigned to the lowest order of slaves. Rabbis were forbidden to require their students to rinse their feet.

At this particular meal Jesus was the host. He had no slave to perform this humiliating service. Certainly, the proud, self-seeking apostles would not stoop to rinse one another's feet. So Jesus, the host, did it for them.

John A. Broadus was one of the leading New Testament scholars of his time. At that time, it was customary for a guest, upon retiring for the night, to place his or her shoes outside the door of the guest room. During the night a servant would take the shoes, shine them, and return them to the guest's door.

On one occasion, a man was an overnight guest in the Broadus home. Just before retiring for the night, he placed his shoes outside the door. Soon he heard the footsteps of one who came to his door and then walked away. The next morning he again heard footsteps coming to his door. Assuming that it was the servant returning his shoes, he opened the door to get them. A man was stooping down to place the shoes on the floor. Then he stood up. To the guest's great surprise, he stood facing Dr. Broadus. Having no servant, the great scholar had shined the shoes himself. He had caught the spirit of Jesus, and *great people can afford to be humble!*

For, "He riseth from supper, and laid aside his [outer, *ta himatia*] garments; and took a towel, and girded himself" (v. 4). Then pouring water into a bason, he "began to wash [rinse, *niptein*] the disciples' feet, and to wipe them with the towel wherewith he was girded" (v. 5).

How embarrassed the apostles must have been as one by one their Lord rinsed the dust from their feet! If not, they should have been! A service they were too proud to render was being done by their Lord. The fact that John alone recorded this is most significant. With his sensitive soul, he must have been embarrassed most of all. More than a half-century later he had not forgotten it. We are eternally in his debt for preserving it for all time to come.

"Then cometh he to Simon Peter" (v. 6). Just reading this line leads us to expect something out of the ordinary, and we are not disappointed. To this impulsive apostle it was unthinkable that his Lord would perform so humbling a service to him. Apparently Peter was the last one. Otherwise, we would not be surprised had he taken the bowl and towel from Jesus and finished the job for Him.

But as it was, he simply asked, "Lord, dost thou wash [rinse] my feet?" "Thou" is intensive. Literally the question reads, "Lord, you of all people rinse my feet?" It is almost a refusal to permit it. Jesus reminded Peter that he did not really understand the meaning of His act, but later he would know (v. 7). In verse 7, the former "know" denotes perceptive knowledge; the latter refers to experiential knowledge. Peter could not grasp fully Jesus' act of humility, but by experience he would learn it. And he did, as seen in 1 Peter 5:5: "Yea, all of you be subject one to another, and be clothed [gird yourselves] with humility: for God resisteth the proud, and giveth grace to the humble." Like John, Jesus' act made a lasting impression on Peter.

But for the present Peter said, literally, "Not never may you rinse my feet unto the age" or forever. Note the strong double negative that opens the verse and ends with the words expressing eternity. It could not be a more emphatic refusal.

However, Jesus reminded him that if He did not rinse his feet, Peter would have no part with Him. Actually, Peter's attitude at the moment was one of pride. He was proud of his mock humility. But he would never gain true humility as expressed by Jesus unless he submitted to His act.

Peter never did anything halfway, so he went to the other extreme. From refusing to let Jesus rinse the dust from his feet, he asked Jesus to give him a bath thoroughly all over. He did not use the word for "bathe," *louō*, but it is implied. Jesus used it in His reply. I see a slight smile on Jesus' face and a twinkle in His eyes when He said, in effect, "Peter, you were supposed to take a bath before you came. If so, then your body is clean all over. You only need to have the dust rinsed from your feet" (v. 10).

Then Jesus turned from physical to spiritual cleanliness. All the apostles were clean from sin spiritually, except Judas whom Jesus knew to be the betrayer. He had never been cleansed from sin.

It is not easy for Christians to learn the lesson of humility, especially those who have so much of which to be proud.

One day Billy Graham and I were playing golf. I said, "Billy, you amaze me." When asked why, I replied, "You have had enough attention to make a fool out of a thousand men. But the more attention you receive, the humbler you get." He replied, "Since you mention that, I will say that it is at that point that my greatest temptation lies. Everywhere I go they want to put me in a hotel suite and furnish me a large car to drive. To combat pride, I insist upon two plain hotel rooms with a connecting door, one room for me and one for T. W. [Wilson who travels with Billy]." Then he added, "If I ever lose my humility, I don't think I will live long. For God said, 'I am the Lord: that is my name: and my glory will I not give to another, neither my praise to graven images'" (Isa. 42:8).

But Billy has not only learned humility. He practices it. Some years after the above conversation he came to Oklahoma City for a one-night engagement. The day before his arrival I received a call from a lady who said she and her mother were Nazarenes. Her mother was in a nursing home and bedfast. She could only experience religious services by radio and television. And she felt that Billy Graham was her pastor.

Then she said, "I know he will only be here a few hours. But if he could visit my mother, it would crown her life. If he can't go, I will understand. I'm not even mentioning it to her lest she be disappointed."

Billy arrived about 4:00 p.m., and the service was at 7:00 p.m. I told him about the little lady, but I assured him he need not go since he needed to rest.

He said, "Certainly we will go!" When we arrived, she was propped up in bed wearing a beautiful bed jacket. Her snow-white hair was arranged to perfection. I know her daughter had prepared her thus.

Billy led into the room. Taking her hand, he said, "I'm Billy Graham. I have come by to see you!" She looked at him as if to say, "Yes, and I am Josephine." But he repeated what he had said, adding, "I've come to pray with you."

Then she recognized him. Her mouth came open as she gazed at him. It seemed that she could not speak. But then she started talking, and we could not stop her. Finally, Billy said, "Well, let us have a word of prayer." As we left she seemed still in a daze. The next day her daughter called to tell me that visit really did crown her life.

That evening to a packed auditorium of thousands, as I presented Billy, I told this story. Then I said, "Our guest's name is a household word around the world. He has the ear of kings, queens, presidents, and the like throughout the nations. He has preached the gospel to more people than any other man who ever lived, yet after a tiring day, he still has time for one dear little lady in a nursing home." The crowd cheered.

Incidentally, Billy did not want me to tell this story to the crowd: this shows all the more his humility. (The Associated Press carried the story around the world.) In this simple act, Billy showed something of the humble spirit of Jesus. *Great people can afford to be humble!*

The Lesson for Us (John 13:12-17)

After Jesus was seated, He applied the lesson of His act (vv. 12-16). Though He was their Lord, He had rinsed their feet. Surely then, said He, "Ye ought also to wash [rinse] one another's feet." This was not a third ordinance. Jesus did it as an example to show us how we should act toward each other. No service is too low or demeaning but that it glows with heaven's light when done in the name of the Lord. "If ye know these things, happy are ye if ye do them" (v. 17).

One can best judge a person's greatness, not by the great things he or she does, but by the little things. One of the greatest Christians I ever knew was Dr. L. R. Scarborough, president of Southwestern Baptist Theological Seminary, Fort Worth, Texas. In 1941, three years and three months out of Southern Baptist Theological Seminary, Louisville, Kentucky, I became pastor of Emmanuel Baptist Church, Alexandria, Louisiana. Shortly thereafter I received a letter from Scarborough. Since I had come west of the Mississippi River, he wanted me to come to the campus, speak in chapel, and get acquainted with the seminary.

On the appointed day I went to Fort Worth. Embarking from the train, I expected to be met by a secretary or student. But there stood Scarborough. At 10:00 a.m., I spoke in chapel. At 11:00 a.m., we attended revival services at Gambrell Street Baptist Church where he was a member. At noon we ate lunch; following that he gave me a tour of the campus and introduced me to the faculty members. He then took me back to the train. Scarborough taught me many lessons that day. But most of all that *great people can afford to be humble!* Are you?

11
The Other Jesus

(John 14:16-18,26; 15:26; 16:8-14)

"I will pray the Father, and he shall give you another Comforter, that he may abide with you for ever" (John 14:16).

It was Thursday night of Passion Week. By Jewish time it was early on Friday, since the Jewish day began at sunset. Shortly before sunset on Thursday, Jesus and the apostles gathered in an upper room somewhere in Jerusalem. There they ate the Passover meal. During this meal Jesus indicated to John that Judas was the one who would betray Him. This He did by dipping bread in the "sop" or gravy and giving it to Judas. In that day, it was customary for the host at a meal to honor a guest. The other apostles would so interpret this action toward Judas. But John understood otherwise (John 13:24-26). Also Judas likewise understood this gesture. So he left on his mission of betrayal.

John 13:30 notes that "it was night." Of course, it was night, but since it was the time of the full moon, this was not John's only meaning. He spoke of the midnight blackness in Judas's soul (John 13:27).

After Judas's departure, Jesus instituted the Lord's Supper. This Supper is for baptized believers only. Judas most likely had been baptized by John the Baptist, but he was not a believer.

Since the other Gospels had recorded the institution of the Lord's Supper, John omitted it. Instead, he recorded a body of Jesus' teachings following the Supper that the other Gospels do not contain. Our Lord's purpose was to prepare the apostles for the immediate ordeal of the crucifixion and for the time following His ascension.

Who can forget Jesus' memorable words that begin: "Let not your hearts be troubled: ye believe in God, believe also in me" (John 14:1). "Be troubled" describes an ocean caught in the teeth of a storm. A mighty storm was about to break upon them.

In these and following words, Jesus gave the secret of an untroubled heart. It was not the philosophy of the Stoics who taught that one should steel one's emotions, grin and bear it, and ride out the storm of trouble. Nor was it the philosophy of the Epicureans who said to drown your troubles in pleasure. Those who try it find that trouble can swim and multiply in the process. Jesus' secret is faith— faith in God the Father and faith in God the Son.

Running throughout John 14—16 is the theme of our Lord's abiding presence in the Person of God the Holy Spirit. It is the purpose of this message to examine this promise concerning the indwelling of the Holy Spirit and His enabling power both in the early church and in our Christian fellowship and work today.

The Promise of the Spirit (John 14:16-18)

In these verses Jesus looked beyond His sojourn on earth. For about three and one-half years, Jesus' disciples had relied on His physical presence. In the future they must rely on His spiritual presence.

After He returned to the Father, Jesus promised, "I will pray the Father, and he shall give you another Comforter, that he may abide with you for ever; Even the Spirit of truth; whom the world cannot receive, because it seeth him not, neither knoweth him: but ye know him; for he dwelleth with you, and shall be in you" (vv. 16-17).

Note that praying for the Spirit to come is not our responsibility. Jesus said that He would pray the Father, and He would give us "another Comforter." This promise was fulfilled in the coming of the Holy Spirit at Pentecost. There is no scriptural mention of the Spirit being taken from the world. Our prayer should be that we will submit to His presence and power for He abides with us forever.

Jesus called Him "another Comforter" and identified Him as "the Spirit of truth." But the focus is on "another Comforter." "Comforter" renders a Greek word that has come into English as "Para-clete." It means "one being called alongside." It might mean "Comforter" or "Encourager." As a legal term, it was used of a law-yer who stood alongside a client in court, especially a lawyer for the defense. In 1 John 2:1 it is translated as "advocate," the Latin equiva-lent of the Greek word. Thus on earth He is God's Advocate before us. In heaven, in the Person of Christ, He is our Advocate before God. In Romans 8:9, the Spirit is called both the Spirit of God and the Spirit of Christ. There are so many shades of meaning in Para-clete, but a good translation is "Divine Helper."

But note the word "another." This translates a Greek word mean-ing "another of the same kind." In other words, another Helper of the same kind that Jesus had been. B. H. Carroll called the Holy Spirit "the other Jesus." All that Jesus had been to His people while on earth, He will continue to be through His Spirit.

Now as the world system that refused to acknowledge God did/ does not receive Christ, so it cannot receive His Spirit. It neither sees nor knows Him by experience, but the Christian knows Him be-cause, literally, "alongside you he keeps on dwelling, and in you he will continue to be."

Did you catch that? The moment you received Jesus as your Savior He indwelt your life. And He will continue to be in you. Again in Romans 8:9 Paul said, "Now if any man have not the Spirit of Christ, he is none of his." Such a person is not even a Christian. In the Book of Acts, each time that the Holy Spirit is seen coming on an individ-ual person (not on the church), it is directly related to that person's regeneration experience (Acts 8:17; 10:44; 19:6). It is not some sub-sequent experience or a "second blessing." This is evidence that one has been saved!

When I discovered this for myself, I had a problem with Acts 8. Some days, perhaps at least four, intervened between the Samari-tans' regeneration and the coming of the Spirit upon them. In Acts 10 and 19 it happened immediately. Finally, it dawned on me that in Caesarea and Ephesus an apostle was present to verify that those had received the Spirit. In Samaria the Spirit came after two apostles arrived from Jerusalem.

In Ephesians 1:13-14, Paul said that the Spirit indwelling the Christian is God's seal of ownership and His guarantee that the believer is saved and kept saved by God's grace and power.

Furthermore, 1 Corinthians 6:19 says that Christians are "the temple of the Holy Ghost [Spirit] which is in you." "Temple" translates *naos*, used of the holy of holies in the Jewish temple. Also in 1 Corinthians 3:16 he said that the church is the temple *(naos)* of God. As the Spirit indwells each Christian so He indwells the Christian fellowship of believers.

The indwelling of the Spirit is a most solemn truth. It means that wherever we go and whatever we do involves the Holy Spirit. So we should refuse to go anywhere or do anything we would not do if the Lord were present in bodily form.

Since the Holy Spirit is the Spirit of Christ, we should take to heart other of Paul's words in 1 Corinthians 6:15. "Know ye not that your bodies are the members of Christ [parts of His body]? shall I then take the members of Christ, and make them members of an harlot?" It is no wonder that Paul revolted against such an idea with his familiar "God forbid."

But on the brighter side, Jesus said, "I will not leave you comfortless: I will come to you" (John 14:18). "Comfortless" translates a Greek word transliterated into English as "orphans." "I will not leave you [as orphans]." In this one word Jesus expressed the feeling in each apostle's heart.

Thinking of Jesus' departure from the world made them feel like orphans. But He promised that in His Spirit He would come to them.

Have you ever wondered what a privilege it would have been had you lived and walked with Him when on this earth? As strange as it may sound, ours is a greater privilege. He walked alongside the apostles; He dwells in our bodies. They heard Him through their ears; we hear Him in our hearts. There were times when they were away from His presence; we are never away from Him. They walked with Him for about three and one-half years; He abides with us forever.

The Spirit and the Saved (John 14:26; 15:26-27; 16:12-14)

Being indwelt by the Spirit calls on us to "be filled with the Spirit" (Eph. 5:18). We are indwelt by the Spirit at the moment of regeneration. We are filled with the Spirit when we yield ourselves to His power.

Think of yourself as a building. Its wiring is indwelt by electricity. But the electrical power expresses itself only when switches are on so that it performs its work through light bulbs, motors, and other electronic equipment. You are filled with the Spirit's power when you yield yourself to the Spirit to do His work.

Jesus said, "But the Comforter, which is the Holy Ghost [Spirit], whom the Father will send in my name, he shall teach you all things, and bring all things to your remembrance, whatsoever I have said unto you" (John 14:26). The apostles did not fully understand the gospel of a crucified and risen Lord until the Spirit came at Pentecost.

How else can we explain the writing of the Bible apart from the Holy Spirit? Paul said, literally, that "all scripture is God breathed" (2 Tim. 3:16). *God-breathed* translates a word that is a combination of the words for God and Spirit. Furthermore, Peter said, literally, "No prophecy of the scripture is of private origin. For the prophecy came not in old time by the will of man: but holy men of God spake as they were moved [borne along] by the Holy Ghost [Spirit]" (2 Pet. 1:20-21). Since the New Testament was in process of being written, they wrote of the Old Testament. But it also applies to the New Testament.

Admittedly the writers of the Gospels and Acts had access to other accounts of Jesus' ministry (Luke 1:1-4). But the Holy Spirit guided them in their writing.

And the Spirit called to their remembrance things that Jesus had taught them. For instance, though John wrote his Gospel at least fifty years after Jesus returned to the Father, he remembered minute details not found in the other Gospels.

Likewise, how apart from the Holy Spirit can we explain the other

New Testament writings that interpret the deep things of Christ? Jesus said, "I have yet many things to say unto you, but ye cannot bear them now" (John 16:12). They were not ready to bear and understand them. "Howbeit when he, the Spirit of truth is come, he will guide you into all truth" (John 16:13). "Truth" here refers to spiritual truth.

Except for Paul, these writers of epistles and the like were for the most part ordinary men without unusual natural abilities. Through the power of the Spirit, they wrote truth that has challenged the best intellects of the ages. Paul himself insisted that he received his message directly from the Lord. He often spoke of divinely given visions. John "was in the Spirit" when he received the Revelation (Rev. 1:10).

Jesus said that the Spirit would not "speak of himself; but whatsoever he shall hear, that shall he speak: and he will shew you things to come" (John 16:13). The Spirit does not speak of Himself; He reveals Christ. For Jesus said, "He shall glorify me: for he shall receive of mine, and shall shew it unto you" (John 16:14).

Note "He shall glorify me." In the Greek text "me" is emphatic: "Me and no one else will He glorify." This understanding leads me to conclude that any system of theology that magnifies the Holy Spirit above Jesus is not of the Holy Spirit (see 1 John 4:1).

Speaking of the guidance of the Holy Spirit, He also guided in the spread of the gospel. Shortly before His ascension, Jesus told His disciples to remain in Jerusalem—literally, "until ye get yourselves clothed with power from on high" (Luke 24:49). They were to receive power after the Spirit came at Pentecost (Acts 1:8).

Not only were they empowered, but they were guided. In Acts every new development in the spread of the gospel was either at the command or with the approval of the Holy Spirit. He has guided through the centuries, even as He guides today.

In the early 1940s, I was on a committee of the Southern Baptist Foreign Mission Board to nominate a new executive secretary of the Board. At the outset we agreed not to consider anyone then connected with the Board. At that time, M. Theron Rankin was Secretary of the Orient for the Board.

The committee spent a year searching, but in every case considered, there was something that caused us not to interview anyone. Finally, the committee met in the Biltmore Hotel in Atlanta, Georgia, prior to the 1944 meeting of the Southern Baptist Convention. Our chairman, noting our frustration, raised the question of changing our policy on considering employees of the Foreign Mission Board. All of us agreed.

Then the chairman said, "Without mentioning any person's name, let us have a season of prayer. Then let each member write on a piece of paper whatever name he or she feels led to write." When the secretary had read the papers, everyone had written the name of M. Theron Rankin. As I think back over the years, that experience stands out as the most definite one of the leadership of the Holy Spirit. Yes, the Holy Spirit is still to me the Administrator of the Godhead.

The Spirit's Work With the Lost (John 16:8-11)

The Holy Spirit works in and through Christians. He works with the lost to bring them to Christ for salvation. All our eloquence and skill cannot accomplish this. We are to bear our witness concerning Christ. But our efforts are brought to fruition through the Holy Spirit.

Jesus said, "When he is come, he will reprove [convince, convict] the world of sin, and of righteousness, and of judgment" (John 16:8). "Convict" means to expose or bring to light, to refute with a view to correction. Note the three areas of conviction: sin, righteousness, and judgment.

The first area of conviction is sin: "Of sin, because they believe not on me" (v. 9). In light of Jesus' redemptive work, the Spirit will expose the sinfulness of unbelief with respect to Jesus. He will show you the tremendous price God in Christ paid for your sin. If you believe in Jesus on this basis, He will save you from sin. But if you reject Him, then your sin remains, not a sin of ignorance but of full knowledge. And you yourself will have to pay the wages of sin, which is death (Rom. 6:23a) or eternal separation from God. The only sin of which you cannot be forgiven is a full, final unbelief in Jesus (John 3:18).

The second area of conviction is righteousness: "Of righteousness, because I go to my Father, and ye see me no more" (v. 10). "Righteousness" is used in three ways. It is what God is in His nature. It is what He demands in us, but we cannot achieve it within ourselves. For this reason it is what God provides for us in Christ as an expression of His grace.

In His life, Jesus perfectly revealed and lived God's righteousness. In His death and resurrection, He took our place to provide righteousness for us. Now that Jesus has returned to the Father, the Holy Spirit continues to reveal this to us. But if we reject Christ, saying that we will achieve this righteousness by our own efforts, we fail to receive the righteousness of God that is in Christ (Rom. 10:3-10).

The Greek word for righteousness belongs to a family of nouns ending with the Greek letter *eta* (long *e*). This denotes that in Christ we personally are not righteous. But God chooses to regard us as such. When He looks at us He sees, not our unrighteousness, but the righteousness that is in Christ. It is thus that we are saved from sin.

The final area of conviction is judgment: "Of judgment, because the prince of this world is judged" (v. 11). "Is judged" means "a complete, final judgment." If you believe in Christ, you have already been judged through His atoning death. But if you reject Him in favor of Satan, then you personally face the judgment he has received. If you do this, it is your own choice. So you have no excuse before God.

Thus we may sum it up in the following words: the Holy Spirit convicts us of sin that we have, of God's righteousness that we do not have, and of the final condemning judgment that we most certainly face apart from Jesus Christ. So God has done all that even He can do to save us. He sends no one to hell of His own accord. If we go to hell, we choose to do so on our own.

The early American preacher Jonathan Edwards was famous for his sermon "Sinners in the Hands of an Angry God." He pictured sinners dangling over the fires of hell, held only with one thin spider's web. As lost people heard it, they screamed out for mercy. But what they often overlooked is that the preacher pictured that spider's web as the grace of God. Only God's grace prevents us from falling into hell.

One further thing needs to be said about this "other Jesus." Not only does He convict, but He gives us the ability to repent and believe in Jesus as our Savior. Furthermore, Jesus said that we must be born of the Spirit in order to enter the kingdom of God (John 3:3). So I like to think of the Holy Spirit as the attending physician as each believing soul is born into the kingdom of God.

Do you feel an urge to trust in Jesus as your Savior? That is the Spirit of God speaking to you. Do you feel a tendency to delay your open confession of faith in the Savior? That is the spirit of Satan speaking to you.

Every right-thinking person wants to be saved in heaven after the sojourn on earth. The devil respects your intelligence too much to say otherwise. So he says, "Sure! You want to be saved. But not now. Put it off!" And he snares untold multitudes thus. But God through His Spirit is saying, "Today if ye will hear his voice, Harden not your hearts" (Heb. 3:7-8).

Today may be your last day. But even if you continue to live on this earth, you need Christ today. He will give you abundance of life here and now and life without end with Him in heaven. The Holy Spirit says, "Now!" The evil spirit says, "Later!" Which will you heed?

12
Who Was on Trial?

(John 18:13-14,19-24,28—19:16)

"Then led they Jesus from Caiaphas unto the hall of judgment: and it was early" (John 18:28).

The story is told of a man who knew nothing about art. He had wandered into an art museum. As he stood before one of the old masters, he criticized it. He thought it stood on trial before him. But all the time he was on trial before it. Likewise people may criticize, even reject, Jesus as though He were on trial before them, when, in fact, they are on trial before Him.

The trial of Jesus consisted of two phases, one Jewish, the other Roman. Each of these consisted of three parts: the Jewish trial—first before Annas, then before the Sanhedrin before dawn, and before the Sanhedrin after dawn—and the Roman trial—first before Pilate, then before Herod Antipas, and a second appearance before Pilate. John recorded the three Jewish trials, but he omitted the appearance before Herod Antipas.

On that infamous day, Jesus was on trial before the courts of humanity. But in reality those involved in the human trials were on trial before the judgment seats of history and of eternity. This message examines the former in light of the latter.

The Jewish Trial (John 18:13-14,19-24)

Apparently, Judas had fulfilled his agreement to betray Jesus sooner than expected. It was sometime after midnight. The members of the Sanhedrin were asleep. Some time was necessary to assemble them. So in the meantime Jesus was taken before Annas, a former high priest and the father-in-law of Caiaphas the present high priest. Though Annas had been removed from office by the Romans, he still had a great influence with them. Any charge against Jesus by Annas would have great influence with Pilate.

So having arrested Jesus, the temple police "led him away to Annas first" (v. 13). But apparently he failed to get any charge against Jesus (vv. 19-23). He merely asked Him about His disciples and teachings. In reply, Jesus reminded Annas that He had taught openly in the temple and synagogues. None of His work had been done in secret. If Annas himself was unaware of these things, he could ask those who had heard Him.

With this, one of the temple police slapped Jesus, saying that He should not speak in such a manner to the high priest. (Note that Annas still had the title but not the office.) In turn, Jesus rebuked the policeman. He had done nothing to deserve this.

Indeed, Jesus had done nothing to deserve being on trial in the first place. All He had done was to expose the sins of the people and especially those of the Jewish leaders.

I have often reminded young preachers that they can preach against sin all they please without getting into trouble—unless they name it. And they really get into trouble when they apply it. Jesus had both named it and applied it. Even so, underneath this was what these rulers saw as a threat to their position of power over their people. Evil is bad, but entrenched evil is worse.

By this time the Sanhedrin had assembled. So Annas sent Jesus "unto Caiaphas, the high priest" (v. 24). It was during Jesus' appearance before that body that Peter denied Him three times (vv. 16-18,25-27).

Since the other Gospels had reported the Jewish trial, other than the brief episode before Annas, John merely mentioned the fact that Jesus was brought before the Sanhedrin and that this body took Him to appear before Pilate, the Roman procurator.

But the other Gospels show that the proceedings before that body were little more than a kangaroo court. It was illegal in every respect. The one on trial was abused. The trial was held at night. False witnesses were used whose witness did not agree. Under oath,

Jesus was forced to incriminate Himself. In the voting procedures of the Sanhedrin, in order that the votes of the younger members not be influenced by the others, they were to vote before the older ones did. In Jesus' case, Caiaphas himself was the first to vote that Jesus should die (Matt. 26:65-66). Jewish law forbade convicting and sentencing to death on the same day. So after convicting Jesus in a night meeting they adjourned, then met again after daylight to pronounce sentence formally (Matt. 27:1). But according to Jewish time it was still the same day. The entire procedure was "Get the trial over so we can hang him."

We follow such proceedings with disgust. But how many of us arbitrarily reject Jesus on the same or on less evidence? Is it because we do not want to change our life-styles? Why not look ahead and see where your present way of life is leading you?

Do you reject Jesus because you do not understand Him or the gospel? If so, you are trying to be saved through reason and not by grace through faith. If you could fully understand Jesus, you could not worship Him: your mind would be greater than He is. To be sure, both Jesus and the gospel are mysteries to us. But if we remove the mystery from Christianity, we have left only a moral philosophy. Someone defined faith as the ability of the soul to go beyond the point where reason can go.

Do you say that you live only by reason and understanding? Is there no place in your life for faith? The fact of the matter is that everyone has faith. It is simply a question of in whom or what you place your faith. When we are ill and our doctor prescribes a certain medicine, do we understand how it heals us? Or that a particular medicine taken into our stomachs heals a particular part of our bodies? No. It is because we have faith in our doctor's judgment.

In my college pastorate I performed the wedding ceremony for two of our young people. In due time a baby was born. After the mother returned home from the hospital, she died of blood poisoning. People criticized the doctor, but he told the bereaved husband that he could not understand what happened. Then he said, "The prescription I gave her when she came home was to prevent this." The young man's face turned white as a sheet as he pulled a piece of paper from his pocket. It was the prescription. "My God," said he, "I forgot to get it filled!"

So is everyone who, knowing the gospel, does not fill God's prescription for salvation.

The Roman Trial (John 18:28—19:16)

The Roman government vested in the Sanhedrin civil and religious authority. But it reserved to itself authority to impose the death penalty. So even though the Jews and Pilate mutually despised each other, the Sanhedrin had to take Jesus to him for imposing and carrying out the death penalty. John gave a fuller account of the trials before Pilate, adding details omitted by the other Gospels.

Pilate lived in Caesarea, coming to Jerusalem only when necessary. One such time was to be near his troops during a Jewish Passover when nationalistic feelings ran unusually high. Normally when in Jerusalem, he stayed in the palace of Herod the Great. We may assume that he was there at this time.

John 18:28 calls this palace ("judgment hall," KJV) the "Praetorium" (NASB). Among other things, this word denoted the elite praetorian guard in Rome whose primary duty was to protect the emperor. It was also used of the tent of the commanding general of an army in the field. For our purpose, it denoted the residence of a Roman procurator.

Since it was the time of the Passover, members of the Sanhedrin refused to enter the dwelling of a Gentile lest they be defiled. Therefore Pilate came out to them, but Jesus was taken into the palace.

In verses 29-31, we see the antagonism between the Jews and Pilate. In response to his inquiry as to their accusation against Jesus, they said, "If he were not a malefactor, we would not have delivered him up unto thee." To them, Pilate's question was an insult that questioned their authority. Thinking it had to do with religion, Pilate told them to handle the matter. And though it rankled them to admit it, the Sanhedrin reminded Pilate that only he could sentence a man to death. They had not brought Jesus to Pilate for trial but merely to get him to sentence Him to death. John noted that this fulfilled

Jesus' prediction that He would be crucified. Had the Jews put Him to death it would have been by stoning.

So Pilate entered the palace to question Jesus (vv. 33-38). According to Luke 23:2, the Jews had accused Jesus of claiming to be a king and, therefore, Caesar's rival. This was the only charge that interested Pilate. But after a preliminary examination in which Jesus said His was a kingdom of truth, Pilate saw that He posed no threat to Caesar. So he went out and told the Jews that he found no fault or crime in Him worthy of death (John 18:38). It was at this point that he sent Jesus to Herod Antipas (Luke 23:6-12).

Soon Jesus was back before Pilate. Knowing that Jesus was innocent, Pilate resorted to a custom of releasing a prisoner chosen by the people. At that time he held a notorious prisoner named Barabbas. Mark 15:7 describes Barabbas as an insurrectionist, robber, and murderer. He probably had presented himself as a false messiah. Following an unsuccessful attempt at revolution, he escaped to become a robber. In fact, he probably was scheduled to be crucified the next day. Surely, thought Pilate, the people would not want him released, so he offered to release either Jesus or Barabbas. The people chose Barabbas.

Failing at this point, Pilate again attempted to spare Jesus by appealing to the Jews' sense of mercy (John 19:1-5). After scourging Him, the soldiers mocked Him by dressing Him as a king. They made a crown of thorns that pierced His brow. Then bringing Jesus forth to be viewed by the crowd, Pilate uttered his famous words, *Ecce homo*, meaning "Behold the man" (v. 5). But still the crowd shouted, "Crucify him, crucify him" (v. 6). Asking if he should crucify their King, the chief priests said, "We have no king but Caesar (v. 15). Thus they totally rejected Jesus. Furthermore, they said that if Pilate released Jesus, he was not Caesar's friend. This was a veiled threat to report to Caesar Pilate's many cruel and unlawful deeds. So the procurator gave in. He sentenced Jesus to be crucified—after declaring Him innocent! The vaunted Roman justice trailed in the dust that day.

At this point it is well to note Pilate's many efforts to get Jesus off his hands. He tried to shift the responsibility of judging Jesus onto the Sanhedrin (John 18:31). He endeavored to do the same to Herod Antipas (Luke 23:6-12). He declared Him to be innocent (John 18:38). He tried to substitute Barabbas for Jesus (Matt. 27:17-21). He sought to appeal to the Jews' sympathy (John 19:8-14). But none of these succeeded. Pilate still had Jesus on his hands.

No matter how we may try, we cannot escape a decision concerning Jesus. We meet Him in every life situation. It is impossible to ignore Him. To try to do so is to reject Him. Thus 'as Jesus stands before you, you must decide what you will do with Him. It is either receive Him or reject Him. Which will it be?

Symbolically, Pilate washed his hands of guilt (Matt. 27:24). Said he, "I am innocent of the blood of this just person: see ye to it." The Jewish people replied, "His blood be on us, and on our children" (v. 25). What an awful burden to assume! What a terrible legacy to leave for their children!

But the guilt does not stop there. In crucifixion it was customary to place above the victim's head a board on which was written the crime for which that person was crucified. "Pilate wrote a title, and put it on the cross. . . . JESUS OF NAZARETH THE KING OF THE JEWS" (John 19:19). So Jesus died as a King.

Only John noted that it was written in Hebrew, Greek, and Latin (v. 20). Hebrew or Aramaic was the language of Palestine. Greek was practically a universal language. Latin was the official language of the empire. But John was a mystic, and often we must look beneath the surface to discover his meaning.

G. Campbell Morgan noted that Hebrew was the language of religion. Greek was the language of culture. Latin was the language of government. He noted that these three streams of life flowed together at Calvary. Institutional religion rejected Jesus, pagan culture ignored Him, and institutional government crucified Him. Yes, we were all there when they crucified the Lord.

During the Vietnam war, I read the following story. In the South Pacific there were two American soldiers. One was a Jew, and the other was of Italian descent. The Italian insisted on calling the Jew a Christ killer. When the chaplain heard about it, he called the Italian boy in for a conference. He suggested that they review some Bible history. Said he, "The Jewish Sanhedrin declared Jesus guilty of a capital offence, did it not?" To which the young man said yes. "But it was Pilate, the Roman procurator, who sentenced Jesus to death, was it not?" Again the young man answered yes. "Now," said the chaplain, "the Romans were from Italy, were they not?" "Yes," replied the soldier. "So they were Italians, were they not?" "Yes." "And you are of Italian descent, are you not?" "Yes."

The the chaplain concluded, "So it seems to me that this Jewish boy is no more a Christ killer because of what his ancestors did than you are a Christ killer because of what your ancestors did to Him." The young man had to agree.

Yes, we were all there when they crucified our Lord! That brings us to our question: Who was on trial?

The Verdict of History

The final verdict concerning Jesus was not rendered on that Friday, the blackest day in history. In the final analysis, that verdict is rendered by history.

It is said that history does not render its final verdict on a man until he has been dead for at least fifty years. In many quarters, Abraham Lincoln was not the most popular man of his generation. But history has declared him to be the greatest of presidents of the United States. So history—not his contemporaries—has handed down the final verdict on Abraham Lincoln.

In an infinitely greater sense, history has rendered the final verdict on Jesus Christ. He has affected history more than any mere individual who ever lived. Paul said that had Jesus' contemporaries known, they would not have crucified the Lord of glory (1 Cor. 2:8).

When Caiaphas put Jesus under oath to tell if He was "the Christ, the Son of God" (Matt. 26:63), he received more than a yes answer. "Thou hast said" was the equivalent of our yes.

But Jesus continued: "Nevertheless I say unto you, Hereafter shall ye see the Son of man sitting on the right hand of power, and coming in the clouds of heaven" (v. 64). Caiaphas tore his clothes as evidence that he had heard blasphemy, but Jesus actually had spoken truth. At the moment, Caiaphas thought that Jesus was on trial before him; in truth, he was on trial before Jesus. Caiaphas would bring Jesus to His death, but God raised Him from the dead. He now is at the right hand of the Father reigning in His mediatorial kingdom (1 Cor. 15:25). And He will return at the end of the age when, in the final judgment, Caiaphas—and all like him—will hear the fateful words, "Depart from me; I never knew you" (Matt. 7:23; see Matt. 25:41).

Jesus stood silently before Pilate, the proud Roman who said, "Speakest thou not unto me? knowest thou not that I have power to crucify thee, and have power to release thee?" (John 19:10). But Jesus said, "Thou couldest have no power at all against me, except it were given thee from above: therefore he that delivered me unto thee hath the greater sin" (v. 11).

Pilate thought he was so great and powerful, when all the while, he was but a bit player in the eternal drama of redemption. Guilty of condemning to death One he knew was innocent? Yes. But he was drawn into this drama because he was procurator of Judea. The greater guilt belonged to those who by evil design handed Jesus over to him to be crucified.

Pilate had his one moment on the stage of history. Futilely, he sought to wash away his guilt. In A.D. 36, he was recalled to Rome and banished to Gaul. Standing in Lucerne, Switzerland, one can see Mount Pilatus. An old tradition says that Pilate's ghost dwells in that mountain. When storms rake across it, his ghost is said to come out and wash its hands in the falling rain. All the while he says, "It won't come off! It won't come off!"

Tradition? Yes. But it illustrates the truth that Pilate thought that Jesus stood on trial before him when in truth, he stood on trial before Jesus. All the scrubbing in time and eternity cannot remove the guilt.

What about the ribald mob about the cross? They, too, shared in the guilt of the crime of the ages; and unless they were cleansed later by the blood of their Victim, they too received His condemnation.

Now let us come nearer to home: What about you who yet waver between faith and rejection concerning Jesus? You may think that

Jesus is on trial before you, but in reality you stand on trial before Him. The decision you reach determines your eternal destiny. In the arena of human history, Jesus Christ is not on trial before anyone. But everyone is on trial before Him.

One of the greatest passages in the Bible concerning Christ Jesus is found in Philippians 2:6-11. Christ was "in the form of God." Yet He did not think it was something to hold on to. For our sake He emptied Himself into the form of a man, even a servant or bond slave. Even more, He became obedient unto the death of the cross, a death so cruel that it was reserved only for the worst of criminals.

Then He suddenly turned to ascend the scale of heavenly existence: "Wherefore God also hath highly exalted him, and given him a name which is above every name: That at the name of Jesus every knee should bow, of things in heaven, and things in earth, and things under the earth; And that every tongue should confess that Jesus Christ is Lord, to the glory of God the Father."

Paul looked beyond Christ's incarnation to the consummation of the age: "Every knee should bow, . . . every tongue should confess." Surely those in heaven will do so. Everyone on earth should do so. Those "under the earth," those in hell, will be forced by the power of God to admit that He whom they rejected is truly the Lord Jesus Christ—God's Son and humanity's Savior. But, alas, for them it will be eternally too late!

You may think that Jesus stands on trial before you, but in reality you stand on trial before Him. While there is still opportunity, bow your knee before Him; confess Him as your Lord and Savior.

Yes, you stand on trial before Jesus. The verdict is yours to make. What will it be?

13
The Gospel in One Word

(John 19:23-30)

"When Jesus therefore had received the vinegar, he said, It is finished: and he bowed his head, and gave up the ghost" (John 19:30).

Who can estimate the contents or the power bound up in one word? Take the words *love*, or *hate*, or *hope*. Words are vehicles by which we transfer ideas from one mind to another.

While on the cross Jesus spoke what we call seven "words." With two exceptions they were sentences. But these exceptions were one word. In John 19:28 He said, "I thirst." In Greek it is one word—*dipsō*. Then in John 19:30 He said, "It is finished." It is also one word—*tetelestai*. And what a message these words contain!

One of the greatest sufferings of crucifixion was caused by dehydration. According to custom, Jesus was crucified naked. Every sunbeam became a leech sucking life-giving fluid from every pore of His body. His fever soared. His head ached. His eyes were as flames of fire. His mouth was dry as dust; His lips became parched and cracked. His tongue swelled, and His vocal cords became inflamed. His voice was raspy, almost a croak.

Near the end of the crucifixion Jesus said, "I thirst." He was not asking for relief for Himself. He was about to utter His shout of victory. He did not want it to be a rasping croak. In it He wanted the sound of a trumpet. So He asked for some liquid to cool His vocal cords momentarily. A soldier dipped a sponge in sour wine drunk by soldiers when on duty. Placing it on a reed he pressed it to Jesus' lips. And with moistened vocal cords He uttered the cry, *Tetelestai!*

In Greek there is a family of words that begin with *tele*, which denotes a goal. They come into English in such words as *telephone* and *telegraph*. These mean the voice or writing projected to a distant goal.

In this family were two verbs: *teleioō* and *teleō*. *Teleioō* means to reach a goal or to accomplish a task. *Teleō* means to perform the final act in accomplishing a task or reaching a goal. It is like writing the last word of a poem or driving the last nail in building a house. The latter is the verb in our text—*Tetelestai*. It is a perfect tense of completeness. In effect, Jesus said, "I have completely performed the last act in accomplishing my redemptive work."

Some years ago I was asked to write a book on the seven sayings of Jesus from the cross. I called it *The Crucial Words from Calvary*. So checking all books in my library on these sayings, I found that most of them said the same thing in different words. Therefore I reasoned, "Why write another book saying the same thing?"

It occurred to me to study these words in the Papyri. This word is the plural of *papyrus* (paper), writing material made from the papyrus plant. This body of material contains receipts, bills, letters, legal and commercial documents, and the like of the time when the New Testament was being written. In other words, it was the language of everyday life.

Greek scholars recognized that the Greek of the New Testament was different from that in the Greek classics. The former was simply called New Testament Greek. One German scholar called it the language of the Holy Ghost. His idea was that it was a special language of the Holy Spirit for writing the New Testament.

But one day Dr. Adolf Deissmann of Berlin discovered that the language of the papyri and the New Testament were the same. It was the language spoken in everyday life—common *(koinē)* Greek. Since then the language of the New Testament has been called *Koinē Greek*. All but about forty-five words in the New Testament have been found in the Papyri. Probably these forty-five words were coined by the New Testament writers to express an idea. Paul especially did this. Deissmann's discovery has cast great light on the understanding of the New Testament.

So I thought: *What did these words mean to people then when they first heard or read them in a Christian context?* This proved to be a fruitful study. It was especially true of the word *tetelestai*, "It is finished." I point out three such examples.

A Promissory Note

In ancient times, a man signed a promissory note: on a certain date, "I will pay" a specified sum of money. In Philemon 18-19 Paul, in effect, signed such a note: "I will repay it." But he added, "Albeit I do not say to thee how thou owest unto me even thine own self besides." Apparently, Paul had led Philemon to Christ. In a subtle way Paul said, "I will repay any loss Onesimus may have caused you. But in light of how much you owe me, you are an ingrate if you let me pay it."

In the papyri, examples of promissory notes were introduced by the phrase, "I will pay you this sum." When the note was paid, the receipt was introduced by the word *tetelestai*, the very word used by Jesus on the cross for "It is finished."

Revelation 13:8 refers to Christ as "the Lamb slain from the foundation of the world." Even before God created human beings, He knew that they would sin and need a Savior. Since "the wages of sin is death" (Rom. 6:23), someone must die—the sinless for the sinful. Forgiveness was in God's heart before sin was in the human heart. The redemptive work in eternity had to be wrought out in time in order that lost people might know and believe in the Redeemer.

Thus, in effect, in eternity God the Son signed a promissory note: "I will pay the price for man's redemption." This is expressed by the author of Hebrews (10:5-7) as he put together sayings from the Psalms. (This was an accepted literary pattern in the first century.) "Wherefore when he cometh into the world, he saith, Sacrifice and offering thou wouldest not [did not desire], but a body thou hast prepared me: In burnt offerings and sacrifices for sin thou hast had no pleasure. Then said I, Lo, I come (in the volume of the book it is written of me,) to do thy will, O God."

And now, the virgin-born Son of God, having completely fulfilled

God's will in His life, endured the agonies of the cross for human sin. Having performed the last act in His role as our Redeemer, He cried, "*Tetelestai!* It is finished! The promissory note has been paid!"

The Title Deed

In the Papyri, *teleioō* is found in the sense of executing a deed to property. It was placed in force by dating and signing it. This final act in doing so would be expressed by *teleō*, the verb for "It is finished." This word would express the idea that the deed was fully executed and was fully in force.

I am often asked how the people in the Old Testament were saved. Of course, not all in the Old Testament era were saved, even as all in the New Testament period are not saved. But those saved in the Old Testament time were saved by looking forward in faith to Jesus' atoning work, even as we are saved looking back to it in faith.

Jesus said, "Your father Abraham rejoiced to see my day: and he saw it, and was glad" (John 8:56). The prophets pointed to Christ's coming. Isaiah especially pictured Him as the Suffering Servant (Isa. 42—53). In Psalm 22, David vividly described the crucifixion. Of course, all these prophesied by the Holy Spirit. But the Spirit also enabled those who heard/read the prophecy to catch a gleam of God's redemptive purpose in Christ.

But since these Old Testament worthies were saved prior to Calvary, they were saved *on credit*. The promissory note had not been paid. The deed to their place in the "house of many mansions" had not been dated and signed. As we would say it, had these conditions not been fulfilled, they could be evicted from heaven.

From the beginning of His ministry, Jesus had taught in a veiled fashion about His death. Six months before His crucifixion, near Caesarea-Philippi, He began to teach plainly about it (Matt. 16:21). And Peter rebuked Him for it! In the first century, the Jews were looking for a political-military messiah. Their expectations had no place for a dying or Suffering Servant Christ.

Note that Jesus "began to shew" and Peter "began to rebuke" Him (Matt. 16:21-22). This means that at a given point, Jesus "began to keep on showing" about His death, and Peter "began to keep on rebuking" Him (my translation). It is possible that this continued for the following week. Luke 9:28 says that after eight days Jesus' transfiguration took place. Luke also noted that "as he prayed, the fashion of his countenance was altered, and his raiment was white and glistering" (9:29). Matthew 17:2 says that Jesus "was transfigured before them: and his face did shine as the sun, and his raiment was white as the light."

For what was Jesus praying? The apostles had become so accustomed to Jesus' bodily presence that they saw Him only in His humanity. They even argued with Him. It seems logical that He was praying that the Father would give these followers of Jesus an experience so as to show forth His deity-humanity.

In answer to His prayer, Jesus was transfigured so that His face shone "as the sun." This suggests not only brightness, but that this was not a reflected light such as that of the moon. As the sun shines out of its very nature, so did Jesus' countenance shine. This brightness even came through His clothes. It was Jesus' deity turned up to full power as it shone forth from within. Peter, James, and John saw Him as He is—deity-humanity.

For our purpose, note that they saw Jesus talking to Moses and Elijah. The former symbolized law; the latter symbolized prophecy, or the Hebrew Scriptures. They were talking about Jesus' "decease" (Luke 9:31) or "exodus" out of the world. This involved His crucifixion, resurrection, and ascension. In other words, the Hebrew Scriptures taught the same thing that Jesus was teaching and to which the apostles objected.

Now, not for a moment did Jesus think about avoiding the cross. But I like G. Campbell Morgan's suggestion as to what Jesus, Moses, and Elijah discussed. What would happen if Jesus did not go to the cross? All Old Testament worthies, including Moses and Elijah, were in heaven *on credit*. The promissory note had not been paid. Their deeds to a place in heaven had not been dated and signed. So if Jesus did not go to the cross, *heaven would be emptied,* and *hell would be filled*!

But Jesus *did* go to the cross to pay the price for human sin. On that cross, He dated and signed the deed of everyone in heaven. It is dated fifteenth of Nisan, A.D. 30, and it is signed in His own precious blood. Also, He signed such a deed for all who will believe in Him as Savior. Yes, He signed one for you. But you must claim it for yourself as you trust in Him for your salvation.

The Successful Mission

The Papyri also include the instructions of a father to his son as he sent him on a mission. As the son departed, his father said, "Until you accomplish this for me." He used the word *teleō*, meaning "until your perform the last act in performing this mission." Assuming that the son did this, upon his return his report would be our word *tetelestai*.

In like fashion, the Heavenly Father sent His Son into the world on a mission of redemption. When Jesus said, "I thirst," the last prophecy concerning His death had been fulfilled (Ps. 22:14-15). It was then that Jesus cried, "It is finished" *(tetelestai)*.

On the night before His death Jesus prayed what is called His High Priestly Prayer (John 17). In it He said to the Father, "I have finished the work which thou gavest me to do" (v. 4). Here the verb for "finished" is *teleioō*. This expresses the idea of completing the task. He had fully revealed the Father to the people. About Him He had gathered a small body of believers, but one final act remained as He revealed the Father as redeeming Love. He did this in His death on the cross. With that final act accomplished, just before His death He cried, "It is finished [and finished forever]." Thus the Son reported to the Father: "and he bowed his head, and gave up the ghost" or His spirit.

It is significant how the Gospel writers describe Jesus' death. Both Mark and Luke said literally that He "breathed out" or "expired." John said that He "gave [alongside]" or handed over His Spirit. Matthew is the "Gospel of the King." He said literally, "He dismissed His spirit." When He had performed the final act of His redemptive mission, in effect Jesus said to His spirit, "You can go now." King all the way! "No man taketh it [my life] from me, but I lay it down of myself" (John 10:18).

Matthew 27:36 says that the mob about the cross sat down to

watch Jesus die, but others also were watching. Only, they watched from heaven.

First, there were the twelve legions of angels of which Jesus spoke at His arrest. A Roman legion contained six thousand soldiers. So, seventy-two thousand angels were watching. One cry for help from Jesus, and they would have swooped down to rescue Him from the cross. But that cry never came. Nevertheless, they were watching.

Second, there was the host of Old Testament saints who were in heaven on credit. Most certainly, they were listening. Their remaining in heaven was involved in what was happening at Calvary.

Call it imagination, if you will. But I call it holy imagination. Knowing what was at stake for them, I see them holding in one hand an unpaid promissory note and in the other an undated and unsigned deed. Their hands were held to their ears to enable them to hear better. They were listening for Jesus' cry of victory.

Surely the Father was listening—because His Son was in the final throes of His mission. And then all heaven heard it! "*Tetelestai!* It is finished!" The promissory note had been paid. The deeds to a place in the Father's house had been dated and signed! Nevermore needed the Old Testament worthies to fear eviction!

So they took up the cry: "*Tetelestai! Tetelestai!*" And the angels joined in the cry: "*Tetelestai!*" Up and down the corridors of heaven, reverberating from one end of heaven to the other: "*Tetelestai! Tetelestai!* It is finished."

The Father heard and smiled. To the end, to the last act, Jesus was still His beloved and well-pleasing Son.

Thus we have the gospel in one word. Jesus voluntarily gave His life to redeem a lost humanity. But for His redemption to avail for you, you must personally believe in Him as your Lord and Savior. He paid the price for your sin. He executed in your name a deed for permanent residence in the Father's house. But you must receive it voluntarily for yourself. Otherwise, insofar as you are concerned, Jesus might just as well never to have died on the cross.

God in Christ has done all that even He can do to save you, but He will not destroy your personhood by forcing His redemptive will upon you. The final decision is yours to make. What will it be?

14
Doubting Thomas?

(John 20:19-29)

"But Thomas, one of the twelve, called Didymus, was not with them when Jesus came.

"The other disciples therefore said unto him, We have seen the Lord. But he said unto them, Except I shall see in his hands the print of the nails, and put my finger into the print of the nails, and thrust my hand into his side, I will not believe" (John 20:24-25).

Several years ago the noted news broadcaster Lowell Thomas, Sr., spoke to the Men's Dinner Club in Oklahoma City. During a question-and-answer period, someone posed the following question: "Mr. Thomas, during your career you have known most of the present-day world's great people. Who is the greatest person you have ever known?"

Thomas began his answer by relating the person's many accomplishments and services, including the presidency of the United States. Then he said, "The greatest person I ever knew was Herbert Hoover."

A murmur of surprise went through the audience because popular opinion associates Hoover's name with the depression of the 1930s. In fact, he was no more its cause than anyone else. He happened to be in the White House when it began. A lifetime of selfless service to humanity is eclipsed by one circumstance.

When I was a boy, I attended a country school. Often, at recess the boys played a game. Two boys would wrestle. The object of the game was not to stay on top but on the bottom of the opponent because the other boys, armed with sticks, stood in a circle about the wrestlers, beating the one on top. We called it "The Man on Top Gets the Beating." President Hoover was on top, so he got the beating or blame.

However, strange as it may seem, a quirk of human nature leads us to label a person by some event or a characteristic in his or her life. Such a victim of this tendency is the apostle Thomas. As we all know, Doubting Thomas is a commonly heard epithet. But there are other facets of his nature that are for the most part forgotten.

For instance, Jesus told the twelve He was going to Bethany when Lazarus died. The apostles reminded Him of the Jewish leaders' purpose to kill Him. When Jesus still insisted on going, only Thomas said, "Let us also go, that we may die with him" (John 11:16). But did you ever hear him called Loyal Thomas or Heroic Thomas? On the night before His death, Jesus told the apostles that He was going away, but they knew the way to Him. It was Thomas who asked, "Lord, we know not whither thou goest; and how can we know the way?" (John 14:5). Did you ever hear him called Inquisitive Thomas? To both of these questions the answer is no. He is known only as Doubting Thomas.

This sermon examines the matter of doubt and how it relates to Thomas and to us.

The Definition of Doubt

From its derivation from other languages, doubt is related to correction in learning. It thus means "to hesitate" or "to be uncertain with regard to new opinions or even new truths." Reduced to its basic meaning, doubt is a God-given protective mechanism. For instance, if you tell me that drinking poison will not hurt me, I will doubt you. If you deny that Jesus Christ is the virgin-born, crucified, and risen Son of God, I will doubt you. Doubt is bad when we remain in it, allowing it to fester and deteriorate into cynicism or agnosticism. But without a wholesome doubt, you become a helpless prey to every kind of evil.

Years ago in the seminary, Dr. W. O. Carver taught us how to deal with new ideas or thoughts. He likened it to going to a doctor's office. First, you sit in the waiting room. Then a nurse invites you into a smaller, inner room. Finally, you are received in the doctor's office.

When you meet a new idea, neither accept nor reject it immediately. Tell it to sit in the outer waiting room while you examine it generally in light of what you know to be true. If you find that it does not measure up, reject it. But if you are not certain, then invite it into the smaller room for a more detailed examination. If it fails there, reject it. But if it stands up there, then invite it into your storehouse of truth. It is in light of this example that I invite you to think with me about the experience of Thomas.

The Problem of Thomas (John 20:19-25)

Following Jesus' crucifixion, the disciples feared further reprisals against them. Having tasted blood, so to speak, the Sanhedrin might hound them to their death. So, apparently, they had made themselves scarce in Jerusalem.

Following His resurrection, Jesus had appeared to Mary Magdalene and other women (Matt. 29:9-10). He also appeared to Peter and two other disciples on the road to Emmaus (Luke 24:33-35; 1 Cor. 15:5). But other than Peter, the other apostles had not seen Jesus alive following His resurrection.

On the night of resurrection Sunday, the apostles and the Emmaus disciples were assembled in a room with the doors securely shut. Suddenly, Jesus appeared in their midst. Thinking that He was a spirit, they were terrified. So Jesus gave them the standard Hebrew greeting, "Peace be unto you" (v. 19).

Further to assure them, He showed them His hands and side: marks of His crucifixion. Luke 24:41-43 says that He even ate some broiled fish to show them that He was flesh and bones.

Further pronouncing peace on them, Jesus gave them a commission: "As my Father hath sent me, even so send I you" (v. 21). Then breathing upon them, He said, "Receive ye the Holy Ghost [Spirit]" (v. 22). The verb form of "receive" means "begin to receive." A. T. Robertson called this a prelude to Pentecost when the Spirit came upon the church in power.

John 20:23 poses a problem. Does it mean that Jesus gave them power to forgive or not to forgive sin? Hardly so. This must be interpreted in light of the overall Scripture. Without going into the mechanics of interpretation (see Matt. 16:19), the sense is that as Jesus' *sent ones*, He made them stewards of the gospel. If they preached it, many would hear, some would believe, and heaven has decreed that all who believe it will be saved. If they do not declare it, heaven has decreed that there is no other way by which people can be saved. It is a great privilege to be the custodians of the gospel, but it is an even greater responsibility.

We now come to the heart of our problem. Thomas, called Didymus (a twin) was not present (v. 24). Why? John does not say. He may have had a good reason for being absent. When those present later told him of their experiences, he said, "Except I shall see in his hands the print of the nails, and put my finger into the print of the nails, and thrust my hand into his side, I will not believe" (v. 25). Thomas used a strong double negative. "I will not never believe." For this one statement, history has branded him as Doubting Thomas. But is this a fair assessment of the man?

First, he did not say, "Under no circumstance will I believe that Jesus is risen from the dead." Instead, he set forth conditions necessary for him to believe. After all, this was a world-shaking matter.

Second, he only asked for the proof the others already had.

Third, Thomas knew some things to be true. From a distance he saw the nails driven into Jesus' hands. Also he saw the spear thrust into His side. He knew these to be absolute facts. "Now," said he, "this revolutionary event of which you have told me must agree with things I know are true." He was simply following the procedure set forth by Dr. Carver.

Fourth, Thomas was expected to be a witness concerning these things. Witnesses are supposed to testify only to the evidence they know from personal experience to be true.

Thomas was not to say I *suppose*, I *heard*, or I *think* it to be true. He had to be able to say, "I *know* from personal experience that He who was crucified is alive again." Now we might call him Cautious Thomas, but not Doubting Thomas. He had no more doubts than the others had before they were erased by personal experience.

A witness was on the stand in court. To the lawyer's question, he said, "I think." The lawyer interrupted him. "You are not to think! Just answer the question." The witness turned to the judge. "But, your honor, I am not a lawyer. I can't talk without thinking." With apologies to attorneys, the lawyer was correct. As Sergeant Friday of TV fame used to say, "Just the facts, ma'am, just the facts!" Thomas had to have the facts.

The Confession of Thomas (John 20:26-29)

The following Sunday night Jesus again appeared to the apostles (v. 26). This time Thomas was present. Again, the doors were thoroughly shut. Suddenly, Jesus appeared in their midst with the customary Hebrew greeting, "Peace be unto you."

I have often said that in His resurrection body Jesus could go through closed doors without opening them. It is true that His body now was not subject to the degrees of time, space, and density. But, recently, I discovered that the phrase "vanished out of their sight" (Luke 24:31) may also read that Jesus became invisible to the disciples of Emmaus. This suggests that Jesus' appearing to the apostles with the doors shut could also mean that He became visible. If so, then He could have been present all the time, yet invisible. Then, suddenly, He became visible. If so, it sheds light on verse 26.

Without delay, Jesus said to Thomas, "Reach hither thy finger, and behold my hands; and reach hither thy hand, and thrust it into my side: and be not faithless, but believing."

How did Jesus know about Thomas's demand? Insofar as the record shows He had had no contact with any of the apostles since being with them the previous Sunday night. Was He present but invisible when Thomas made his demand? Or was it due to divine knowledge? In any case, He invited Thomas to do what he said he must do before he would believe that Jesus was risen from the dead.

Jesus did not fear inspection. Instead, He invited it. Neither does Christian truth fear to do battle with error or doubt. Honest doubt when exposed to truth will produce a stronger faith.

This was true in the case of Thomas. Once he recognized Jesus, he did not touch His body. Instead, he confessed, "My Lord and my God" (v. 28). Thomas is the only person recorded in the Gospels who called Jesus "God." Doubting Thomas? Instead he should be called: Thomas the Great Confessor. Furthermore, because Thomas struggled through honest doubt to unquestioned assurance, he has given us one of the greatest proofs of Jesus' bodily resurrection. Charles Kingsley reminds us that we should not fear doubt so long as we have a disposition to believe. Thomas was such a person.

However, Jesus went one step further. He said, "Thomas, because thou hast seen me, thou hast believed: blessed are they that have not seen, and yet have believed" (v. 29). John was the first of Jesus' followers to believe in Jesus' resurrection before he saw Him alive. So this is an obvious reference to John. How he cherished this word from the Lord! Through more than a half century he had carried it in his heart, and he recorded it, not only as a blessed memory but as encouragement to those who have read it across the centuries.

We are in debt to Thomas more than we can express. Many who struggle with doubt and/or a suspended faith with respect to Jesus are encouraged to work through such to a glorious confession of faith in our crucified, risen, and living Savior.

We are even more in debt to John. Of course, he is in a class by himself. He believed before seeing Jesus alive, but he also believed without the testimony of others who had seen Him who was dead and, behold, is alive forevermore.

You and I cannot see Jesus in the flesh, but we have the time-tested testimony of those who did see Him. They were with Him during His ministry, and they were with Him after His resurrection. We have their testimony born out of personal experience.

There are many solid proofs of Jesus' bodily resurrection. For instance, there is the empty tomb. History and critical study have shown that the four Gospels are credible documents. All of them agree that Jesus' body was placed in the tomb on Friday. All agree that the tomb was empty on Sunday morning. Again, Jesus' followers did not expect Him to rise from the dead. Yet they bear witness that He did. Paul spoke of "above five hundred brethren" who at once saw Jesus alive after His death (1 Cor. 15:6). He added that most of them were still living and could give firsthand testimony of the fact.

Following Jesus' resurrection, Sanhedrin bribed the Roman soldiers who guarded the tomb to say that while they slept Jesus' disciples stole His body (Matt. 28:13). This false account falls in upon itself. If the soldiers were asleep, how did they know what happened?

Perhaps the greatest proof of Jesus' resurrection is the Christian movement itself. Look at the difference in the attitude of the early Christians between the crucifixion and resurrection. From acting like scared rabbits hiding in their hole, they became bold as lions facing Jesus' crucifiers. They and multitudes down the ages have died martyrs' deaths for their Lord. Such would be impossible psychologically, to say nothing about spiritually, if it were based on a lie.

But for you, the greatest proof of a living Savior is your personal faith in Him. Often through the years have I heard people say, "When I get the *feeling* I will become a Christian." If you were sick and your physician gave you a prescription, would you say, "When I feel well, I will take the medicine"? Of course not. You take the medicine because you are sick and want to be well. Later you *feel* well because you took the medicine.

In like manner, God has given you a prescription for the fatal disease of sin. That prescription is repentance from sin and faith in Jesus Christ. *Feeling* does not cure your malady. It comes after the cure. Indeed, you are not saved by *feeling* but by *faith*—faith in Jesus Christ as your personal Savior.

Even beyond your initial experience of faith, you know a living Lord as daily you experience His presence. It is an old but true story. A skeptic asked a Christian woman how she knew that Jesus is alive. She replied, "Because I was talking with Him this morning!"